I0610236

Augustine Joseph Hickey Duganne, A. J. H. (Augustine Joseph
Hickey) Duganne

The fighting Quakers

a true story of the war for our union

Augustine Joseph Hickey Duganne, A. J. H. (Augustine Joseph Hickey) Duganne

The fighting Quakers
a true story of the war for our union

ISBN/EAN: 9783337374952

Printed in Europe, USA, Canada, Australia, Japan

Cover: Foto ©ninafisch / pixelio.de

More available books at **www.hansebooks.com**

THE

FIGHTING QUAKERS,

A TRUE STORY OF

THE WAR FOR OUR UNION.

By A. J. H. Duganne.

WITH LETTERS FROM THE BROTHERS TO THEIR MOTHER; AND A FUNERAL SERMON BY

REV. O. B. FROTHINGHAM.

BY AUTHORITY OF THE BUREAU OF MILITARY RECORD.

NEW-YORK :
J. P. ROBENS, 37 PARK ROW.
1866.

TO THE

Mothers of New York State,

WHO GAVE

THEIR SONS TO THE UNION,

This Memoir

IS REVERENTLY INSCRIBED.

INDEX OF CHAPTERS.

EDWARD HALLOCK KETCHAM.

BORN IN MILTON, N. Y., DECEMBER TWENTY-
SEVENTH, EIGHTEEN HUNDRED AND THIRTY-FIVE,
ENTERED THE SERVICE OF HIS COUNTRY, AT
KINGSTON, AUGUST NINETEENTH, EIGHTEEN
HUNDRED AND SIXTY-TWO ; COMMISSIONED
SECOND LIEUTENANT, CO. A., ONE
HUNDRED AND TWENTIETH REGI-
MENT, INFANTRY, N. Y. V. ; KILLED
AT GETTYSBURG, JULY SECOND,
EIGHTEEN HUNDRED AND SIX-
TY-THREE ; BURIED ON THE
BATTLE-FIELD ;
REMAINS SUBSEQUENTLY EXHUMED,
AND RE-INTERRED IN THE
FRIENDS' BURIAL GROUND.,
AT MILTON, N. Y.

JOHN TOWNSEND KETCHAM.

BORN IN JERICHO, L. I., JANUARY TWELFTH, EIGH-
TEEN HUNDRED AND THIRTY-EIGHT ; ENTERED
THE SERVICE OF HIS COUNTRY, IN NEW
YORK CITY, FEBRUARY SIXTH, EIGHTEEN
HUNDRED AND SIXTY-THREE ; COMMIS-
SIONED SECOND LIEUTENANT, CO. M.,
FOURTH REGIMENT CAVALRY, N. Y.
V. ; TAKEN PRISONER, AND DIED
IN LIBBY PRISON OCTOBER
EIGHTH, EIGHTEEN HUN-
DRED AND SIXTY-THREE ;
REMAINS RETURNED TO HIS FRIENDS,
AND RE-INTERRED IN THE
FRIENDS' BURIAL GROUND,
AT MILTON, N. Y.

Memorial.

In the long roll of names made immortal by the war recently closed, there are few around which more interest clusters than those of the brothers KETCHAM. Not that their services were more arduous, or their deaths more heroic, than were those of thousands of others in the Federal ranks, but that they were representatives of a Society which for two centuries has opposed war, strife and bloodshed—the Society of Friends ; and that their names will live as " The Fighting Quakers."

EDWARD H. and JOHN KETCHAM were the sons of DAVID KETCHAM, a native of Long Island, deceased April 2d, 1860, and MARTHA TOWNSEND HALLOCK, a native of Milton, N. Y., and still a resident of that village. Their ancestors, as far back as the family have records, were Friends, or Quakers, and bore their testimony consistently and zealously to all the peculiarities of that Society. They were-well educated and well-read young men, and especially so for what the world would call " mere farmers." With home and plenty around them, and a loving mother to lead them, they grew up to manhood, strong in the faith of their fathers. Thus peacefully pursuing their rural occupations, the youths dwelt with their mother. Thus the rebellion found them. They were opposed to war—they were opposed to slavery; but from the outset their convictions were firm that the war was from God, for the extermination of slavery. Both wished to enlist; but they were loving brothers, and each thought that the other should remain on the farm with their mother. This amicable dispute was gravely and privately settled between themselves, by lot, and Edward, the eldest, gave in his name to the new regiment then being raised in Ulster county.

But, the conscience of John was not satisfied. He felt and wrote, "I ought to give my life, if it be my lot, for the cause of law and liberty in its need;" and, with this impression, he speedily followed his brother as a soldier in the ranks of what to his enthusiastic spirit, was indeed "the army of the Lord."

There is something noble in a faith—no matter what that faith may be—which leads its followers to the stake of the martyr, or impels them to exchange the comforts of home for the privations of the camp and the dangers of the battle-field. It was a faith like this that inspired the QUAKER BROTHERS; leading them in all their marches, sustaining them in all their privations; nerving their hearts on the field of battle, and brightening over their names on the roll of fame, like the light of stars in heaven.

THE FIGHTING QUAKERS.

CHAPTER I.

WAR.

WHEN the Rebellion's defiance was hurled from beleaguring cannon against the ramparts of Fort Sumter; when the flag that surmounted the Federal fortress was lowered before exultant treason; there was but one response from loyal citizens throughout the Republic.

Alike, in mansion and cottage; at the loom of manufacture, the artisan's bench, the student's desk; alike in field and highway, on shore or sea; there was a quick throbbing of pulses, a compression of lips, a bending of brows, as with the spontaneous thrill of an electric current.

Lucifer, as of old, had flung down his gauntlet at the gates of earthly happiness; but Michael, the angel, was ready for the conflict. The evil spirit of Secession was born, but the soul of Union arose to overcome it.

So it was, that while the lightning yet quivered on the wires which bore its intelligence to North, and East, and West, there were "minute-men" already buckling their arms, as in Revolutionary days, there were musterings on village-greens, and marchings to fields of rendezvous, and a hundred thousand brave lives tendered, as offerings on their country's altar.

Then it was, that the valiant "Sixth Regiment of Massachusetts," answering our President's call, strode through the streets of Baltimore, and left its priceless blood upon her pavements.

Then it was, that the brave "Seventh" of New York City—representative of wealth and commerce; and the gallant "Sixty-Ninth," composed of loyal Irish; and the stalwart "Seventy-Ninth," wearing their Scottish tartan; and the bold "Eighth," with the flower of our youth; and the stout Firemen, with Ellsworth at their head; and the noble "Seventy-First," with their dying commander, Vosburgh; and around these, a hundred other generous regiments, from the Hudson to the Lakes, gathered and mustered, with music and banners, until the blue sky of our Empire State was thick with clustering stars, and the winds from all our hills, and the streams in all our vales were vocal with one cry :

"WE COME !"

For the word rang forth that the city of our government was already imperilled by the advance of rebel forces. "The CAPITOL is in danger!" was the startling news which flashed from telegraph to press, and from press to people, in all the borders of our Union. "The CAPITOL is in danger!" was passed from lip to lip, and from heart to heart, until every house-porch, and every hearthstone, and every church, and every school-room echoed the burthen, and the faithful millions of our Nation responded, as with one great voice—

"TO ARMS ! TO ARMS !"

President Lincoln had asked for seventy-five thousand soldiers. He could have enrolled a million, and the Rebellion might, perhaps, have been strangled at its birth. But an all-wise Providence had its own purposes to develop through trial and suffering to the nation. It was necessary that our Republic should pass through a fiery ordeal. Slavery had taken the sword ; it was to "perish by the sword." WAR was ordained as the crucible of our nation, to purge its dross, and to refine its gold.

I have listened often, with hushed heart, to that angelic gospel which was heard of old by the shepherds of Bethlehem, "keeping watch over their flocks by night;" that tender song of Heaven's sweet messengers, who brought " glad tidings of great joy, " proclaiming " on Earth Peace—Good Will to men! "

In all the centuries there have been whisperings of this celestial strain; soft rhythms of perfect love, flowing on like rippling brooks through stormy battle-plains; but, alas! these melodies are evermore drowned by trumpet-blasts, and by the jar and the clash of war-armor.

Thus, from the days when Abram marched forth against banded kings, and when the hand of his first-born Ishmael was against every man; thus, when the Egyptians followed after fugitive Israel; thus, when the trumpets of Joshua were sounded around the ramparts of Jericho; thus, when the Hebrew giant made war on the lords of Philistia; and the Hebrew king lay in wait for the exile David; for ever more the tramp of soldiers echoes from halls of history, and rivers of human blood roll down through the valley of ages!

Thus, I behold in solemn march an endless column of martial spectres; multitudinous armies of all climes and centuries ranged under mouldy banners, keeping step to the monotoned drum-beat of a requiem.   Innumerable hosts of humanity, treading in foot-prints of other hosts, likewise incomputable, but all flanked and guide-marked by grave-hillocks and the ridges and furrows of war fields.

Funereal march!—appalling procession!

Tramp! tramp! through measureless sequences of recorded Time; onward marshaled over forgotten fields of conquest! I hear the hollow resonance of dead foot-falls on causeways paved with glistening skulls, muffled by dust of crumbling bone.

I hear the heavy flap of standards, sodden and crusted with blood. I listen to the dull rumble of war-cars and cannon wheels, to the hoof stamps of chargers, to the creaking of ambulances, to the slow drag of chains on captive feet.

From the East, with Samiel, the desert-wind; swarming like locusts, blackening the white sands, like myriads of grasshoppers! Nimrod, and Belus, and Semiramis, with the armies of Assyria and Babylon; Sethos, and Ramses, and Sesostris, with hosts of triumphing Egyptians; Darius, Cyrus, Cambyses and Xerxes, with numberless Medes and Persians; Hannibals, Alexanders, Constantines, and Mahomets, and Amuraths, with Carthaginians, and Greeks, and Byzantines, and Turkmen; their battling legions banner-led by yellow and green, by arrow and cross, and crescent; traversing grave mounds of drifted sands; climbing mummy-heaps; tumbling over sarcophagi; camping amid stony ruins of empire.

From the West, with chanting of Druid songs, blare of ox-horns, death-dance of yellow-haired

Gauls, and Cymbri, and Ostro-Goths! Brennus and Herrmann ; Roman Cæsars and Antonies ; Frankish Martels and Charlemagnes ; crusading hosts ; red-handed regicides ; Corsican Bonapartes ; tyrants, conquerors, peoples, and despotisms !

From the North, with crash of runic harps, war-songs of vi-kings, hammer-strokes of Thor, and beacon-lights of boreal-auroras ; Sweyns and Si-gurds, Hengists and Harfargars ; Tartars and Russ ; iron-booted Swedes ; following the battle-tracks of Scythian Attilas, and Muscovite Rurics, and Hungarian Arpads, and Sclavonian Sobieskis.

From the South ; great droves of captives, and caravans of war-spoils ; ivory and gold and spices; borne by men slaves, burdened and scourged, and evermore marking their pathways with blood-drippings ; myriads of black-skins, and red-skins, and tawny-skins, branded on breast and backs with tribe-mark and token of foredoomed servitude ; and endlessly crying unto the winds and the waves, and the skies—"How long? how long?"

And the frightful procession—never ending, never halting ; fights on, toils on, through all climes and ages ! Neither from the North, nor the South, nor the East, nor the West, cometh one short hour of respite—one moment's pause in the death-march of warfare and ruin. Century striving after century ; nation crowding upon nation ; blows incessantly falling ; blood always flowing ; human feet forever trampling on human hearts ; fingers clutching sword-hilts ; eyes peering along musket-tubes ; hands busy with bullet-moulds, and cartridges, and bomb-shells.

"As it was in the beginning, is now, and shall be, forever and ever !"

O, Father in Heaven ! is this indeed Thine ordinance ?

It is not for us to answer a question so momentous. God ruleth War ; but it was His voice, also, by the lips of angels, that spake unto the Shepherds of Galilee, and promised them "Peace on Earth—Good Will to Men !"

For it may be, that, in the fathomless design of Infinite Wisdom, these marches and countermarches of mortals have all their place and significance. In the Eternal Harmony of countless spheres, our earthly discords may have rythmic purpose.

Storm-winds and thunders, like flails, beat out the malaria of tropics. War-fields are the threshing-floors of nations, where chaff is parted from wheat, and the grain is made fit for Humanity's garners.

To him who hears aright, the jarring discords of war are not void of harmonious meaning. The crash of shells and roar of cannonry ; the clashing of swords and bayonets ; the blare of bugles and the rattle of drums ; are they not all great chords and stops in the wonderful music of a Divine opera ?

I sometimes fancy that when, at last, the day of our national bridal shall come; when the soul of Freedom shall be married to the body of Union for all time; and when our Republic's anthem, rolling up from chanting millions, shall thrill afar through Old World nations; I sometimes fancy that so grand an oratorio will be hailed by angel-choirs, as a fitting unison of the Eternal "music of the spheres"—which times (as poets tell) the swinging of each new-born world in Heaven's resplendent arches.

Therefore, let us accept even War as an instrument of Omnipotence. If we receive it in Punishment, it is nobler than Pestilence; if it cometh as a Penalty, it is more merciful than the Deluge. But in the Providence of God it may have higher aims and ends than the mere infliction of mortal chastisement. It may work, indeed, through its throes and violences, toward the birth of that pure and perfect Day, when "men shall learn war no more;" when "the sword shall be turned into the plough-share, and the spear into the pruning-hook;" when the "lion shall lie down with the lamb, and a young child shall lead them!"

So, then, abiding still that promised millennium, we may glean from the mighty and terrible engines of war and revolution—from the upper and nether millstones which grind out bloody grain for the   Future's sustenance; we may glean, I say, some sweet examples of ripe manhood—even while we tread beneath our feet the dross of mere brutal ambition.

IT was thus that the great lesson of WAR descended upon that peaceful homestead, where MARTHA T. KETCHAM, the "Quaker" mother, dwelt with her two boys, EDWARD and JOHN. They were the only sons of their mother, "and she was a widow."

For the FATHER, who had reared their infancy—the plain Ulster County husbandman, who kept his testimony through life to the simple faith of "Friends"—had been called to his eternal rest, while yet no presage of her coming trials was revealed to his native country. He had lain down to sleep with "kings and prophets," leaving behind him the record of an upright man, whose humble life and unobtrusive mien were recalled with tender regard, while he was equally remembered for the steadfast rule of righteous dealing which had made him as inflexible in justice as he was quiet in manners.

David Ketcham slept with his ancestry, and the representatives of his name and virtues remained with their beloved mother, whose declining years they hoped to bless by their filial affection and untiring service.

Well educated and of refined feelings, tenderly attached to each other, devoted to their surviving parent, the brothers were fitted to adorn and gladden their home. Tilling the soil of their farm together, and daily interchanging acts of fraternal

kindness, these boys were knit together in soul,
like David and Jonathan.   In comfortable, though
moderate circustances, they were enabled to devote
due time to mutual improvement, and to cultivate
their individual tastes beyond the usual scope of
young men in the country.   They had inherited
honesty, truth and conscientiousness.   They
added to these virtues whatever their hours of
leisure could secure, in mental growth and action.

CHAPTER II.

CALLING TO BATTLE.

GOING back from the Present, with its fresh laurels and green graves, to the Past, with its thorns of trial and blossoms of victory.

Through all these bewildering footprints that cross and recross in the dust of our pavements, I retrace the ancient pathways trodden by sires of the Republic. Out of this maze of masonry which we call the metropolis, I go into " the fields," where McDougal of old spoke burning words to the "Sons of Liberty"—words that became counter-signs of Revolution.

In those days there were no Wall-street brokers to proffer brave loans to a new-born nation ; but there were stalwart men of toil, to beat back the bayonets of hireling soldiery at "Golden Hill." There was no "Committee of Union Defence," to endow an army with the panoply of war; but there were "minute men," each with his trusty gun, to lay both life and goods upon the altar of patriotism.

So from the gallant legions of Our Union, whose tramp yet shakes the massive warehouses of Broadway, I go back, in spirit, to the muster of that first devoted Regiment of New York, whereof ALEXANDER McDOUGAL was colonel, in the days of '76—McDougal, master-spirit of Liberty on Manhattan Island—a brave, unselfish man, of whom Washington said, "HIS zeal is unquestionable;" a loyal soul, whose voice rang forth from prison walls, in fiery vindication of his country's cause.

"I rejoice," said the brave McDougal, "that I am the first sufferer for Liberty, since the commencement of our glorious struggle!"

O Liberty! when shall the man arise whose happiness it shall be to proclaim—"I am the last sufferer for American Freedom!"

For, indeed, there are many battles yet to be waged, and many heroes to fight, and martyrs to die, ere the great bell of our Independence shall find tongue to peal the real meaning of its old inscription:

"Proclaim Liberty throughout the Land, and to all the Inhabitants thereof!"

In the days of our first Revolution, men were moulded in the matrix of a month, and born in an hour, out of the lap of danger. Heroes sprang up full-armed, like fabled offspring of dragon's blood. Therefore it was that, while McDOUGAL was whispering bold thoughts to his Manhattan neighbors, WARREN was counseling with friends at Boston, and the wife of KNOX was hiding her sword under her robe, that it might be ready for Bunker Hill battle.

And far away in the Carolinas, MARION and SUMTER, and MOORE, and the boy ANDREW JACKSON, were listening for Northern echoes to their hearts; while the broad sword of MERCER was unsheathed on Virginian hills, and the claymore of McINTOSH was drawn on the plains of Georgia.

It was then that Marblehead, in Massachusetts, (now dwindled to a fishing town) was rich enough to send her thousand loyal hearts, under bold JOHN GLOVER, to the camp at Cambridge.

Then young OTHO WILLIAMS hastened from loyal Maryland, and drew his maiden sword, that was to flash thereafter on the field of Eutaw, waving the bloody sickle of a bayonet charge, to reap the harvest of victory.

WAYNE and THOMPSON of Pennsylvania; POMROY and NIXON of the Bay State; PUTNAM and WOOSTER of Connecticut; STARK, and "Light Infantry POOR" of New Hampshire; stout ETHAN ALLEN of Vermont; SCHUYLER of New York; SULLIVAN of Maine; GREENE of Rhode Island; are not these noble names still music to our ears? Is not the memory of their bearers still sweet in the garden of glory?

And let us thank God, that everywhere, in the bloody years of our rightful war against treason, the names of such faithful soldiers are recorded upon the pages of impartial history. Not among Generals only—brave and venturous through they be—need we look for examples and models of patriotism. The hero of a knapsack is grand as the hero of a baton. Martyrs ascend to Heaven from rank and file as luminously as from the field and staff. Poor PLUMMER TIDD, who fought with JOHN BROWN at Harper's Ferry, and who lay dying on his cot with deadly fever, while the batteries of Fort Donelson thundered in his ears, was no less a hero than if he had fallen at his sergeant's post in battle. "Is our side winning?" he gasped, as the gunboat rocked beneath him; and when his chaplain answered "Yes," the brave man said "Thank God!" and died.

JOHN BEMAN, the humble watchman of a steamboat, hanged by rebels to a tree in Mississippi, because of being a loyal man, deserves his place upon the hero tablet, not less then our martyred ABRAHAM LINCOLN. "I will die before I take the Southern oath!" this bold Norwegian cried; and they swung his body upward; but his soul soared higher than traitors could reach.

"Don't mind me, boys! Go on with the fight! Don't stop for me!" said Orderly-Sergeant GOOD-FELLOW, at Bethel's fight. He gave his musket to a comrade, and sank dying in his place; a hero-soldier, promoted in death to a rank with GREBLE and WINTHROP, who fell not far from him.

Of such as these are our heroes; and the altars whereon we inscribe their names and modest records are as wide as the battle-fields of our Republic. We are wealthy in these monuments of nationality—these shrines of liberty. The Republic is a temple, based upon, and columned, and walled, and

arched, by such lofty and enduring stones of loyalty. Under and above, and in the midst of departed heroism, our living heroes walk gloriously.

I find no dearth of hero-men in our Republic's
Past; and when the annalists of its latest struggle
shall record the deeds of those who fell, and those
who survived, through the bloody years of Rebellion, there will be columns of fame inscribed with
loyal names that shall blaze like a beacon through
all the Future.

So, then, to the homestead which had descended to them, from maternal ancestors, through a
hundred years; to the widow, who wept over her
husband's recent grave; and to the orphans who
cherished her reverent years; thus, to these "plain
people," and to the simple scenes around them,
our WAR came, with its lessons of mortal and
immortal significance. The same overruling
Providence, that was to summon generals and
admirals to their proud responsibilities, spoke low
into the ears and hearts of two young men, "of
the people called Quakers," and impelled them
away from home and kindred, to render up their
lives in the battles of Liberty.

These "people called Quakers," have done loyal
service heretofore in battles that forever consecra-
ted the soil of our land to freedom. There was a
Quaker, of Rhode Island—GREENE the blacksmith,
"who went forth conquering and to conquer" in
that same South through which many of his descendants have marched to overcome Rebellion.

There were Quakers in Pennsylvania, who sealed
with their blood the holy testimony of religion to
patriotism.   And history has embalmed the memory of those New Jersey "Friends," who knelt
beside HUGH MERCER, after the fight at Princeton,
and received the last sigh of that gallant Scotch-
man, as he died for American Independence.

There are promptings of conscience and mov-
ings of "the Spirit," that are above all method or
professions of religion.   Blessed as is the creed of
"Peace," there may come occasions to its followers,
when the voice of duty will thrill them as with a
trumpet blast, and their souls must leap responsive
to the mandate:

"ARISE, GO UP TO THE BATTLE !"

So, to our young strong men, in their quiet village
of Milton, the voice of duty came with the first news
from Sumter, and it knocked, month after month, at
their hearts, till the eldest arose and girded his
loins for conflict.

He entered his country's service, "for three years
or the war," on the nineteenth of August, 1862, in
the One Hundred and Twentieth Regiment of New
York Infantry, under command of Colonel Sharpe.
Having previously spent some time, assisting to
recruit a company, he was enrolled as a Second
Lieutenant of Company A., at Kingston, in Ulster
County.   His action was the result of a resolution
taken after a close examination of conscience ; and
a resolution once made by the son of David
Ketcham was as unalterable as his sense of right.

His mother wept, and whispered her loving fears of the result; but the brave boy could only answer from his earnest soul—

"No man is too good to die for his country."

And so he turned from the sweet home, and the dear ones beneath its roof-tree. He kept down the choking sob in his bosom, and sought to smile away the doubts and apprehensions that lingered behind him. Who might conceive the depths of a mother's love, and who could measure the burden of her forebodings?

These boys were the hope of their only parent; even as so many thousands of other noble youths were the solace and trust of parents equally fond and devoted. Looking at the parting of this Quaker mother from her first-born marching to war, we may realize the grandeur of patriotism that inspired such multitudes of mothers, in our loyal land, to yield their living jewels for the cause of our Republic. But to this poor mother the whisper of her fears was too prophetic. Not only her first born, but the youngest child of her bosom was to be taken from her, and she was to mourn like Rachel, "because they were not."

CHAPTER III.

ENTERING THE SERVICE.

THE mental and moral excellences of the
brothers Ketcham were not marred by inferior
physical organization.   Both were muscularly de-
veloped, above the medium height in stature, and
of attractive presence as well as handsome features.
Edward's complexion was fair.   His eyes were
blue, his hair and beard light.   John had dark
hair and eyes.   His temperament was more poetic,
perhaps, than that of his brother.   Edward's was
a joyous disposition, quick to appreciate wit, and
to add to it.   John was no less disposed to live-
liness, but his feelings were deep and enthusiastic.
Thus each brother was the other's complement,
and they were equally beloved in the circle of their
friends, equally cherished by their mother.

Severe indeed was the trial to that fond mother,
when her two noble boys wrestled with one
another's affection, and with their great love for
her, as opposed to the duty which each felt that
he owed to their native country.   Strange, indeed,
was it, that, in the ancient homestead bequeathed
by generations of " Friends," these descendants of

a minister of that peaceful society should argue, before that tearful parent, the obligation which they felt that one ought to leave her for the battle-field. But, if they thus departed from the unwar-like faith of their great-grandfather, the Ulster County minister, they kept within their souls the spirit of that godly man, his purity of purpose, and his sympathy with humanity.

"They cast lots!" and the lot fell upon the first-born. Edward was called to put on the armor of patriotism, and he went forth exultingly, in his consciousness of sacred duty.

The mother and her youngest son were left, to follow, from afar, with yearning tenderness, the marches of their absent one; to long for "letters from camp;" to tremble over the news of battles; to commune with one another, in the night-watches, and mingle their reflections through the days; to look at the vacant seat of their beloved; to hope and to pray evermore for his return. It is the story of a myriad of family circles—the record of bereaved homes throughout our land.

Meanwhile, Edward, brave and earnest, was doing his duty manfully; and, week by week, his welcome letters arrived to cheer the waiting ones in his native village. Always loyal and inspiriting, never murmuring, never repining, those simple missives came like doves, "with healing on their wings." In reading their cheerful sentences, one would think that marches and privations, and perils, were but episodes of a tour of pleasant journeying. However arduous his labors, or exposed his service, Edward, the "Quaker soldier," had no complaints to make, and no despondency to indulge in. To use his own terms, he was "all right," wherever and however his duty should call him. "I am well and strong," he wrote, in describing one of his earliest experiences, "and can march through mud, and rain or snow, and come out of it all right. When we were marching the last day, through the mud, I asked the Major how it compared with the hard marching he had seen; and he is an old soldier, and has done hard marching, and fighting, too. He said, "You can set this down as a hard one." Well, if this is a hard one, I can stand it, easily."

Thus, strong-hearted and enthusiastic, the young lieutenant entered upon his country's service. His own letters to his mother and brother will best describe his military fortunes, as well as portray the development of his character.

"MANASSES JUNCTION, Nov. 12th, 1865.

" DEAR MOTHER.—It is now sometime since I have written home, and we have had quite a little experience. To begin with, we were ordered to march on Saturday, first of November. When the order came, I had been sick for three or four days with jaundice—caused by my tent standing on a heap of dirt, deposited by another regiment that had previously occupied the ground. I could always perceive an offensive smell when I came into the tent from the fresh air; suppose, if I had made a fuss about it, I might have had it moved; but I expected the camp would be moved in a few days, as the ground had been condemned by the Doctor. I was not very sick, but sick enough to have it feel a good deal more comfortable to lie down than to sit. We marched about dark, I got my things all ready, and got a lock of hay, and went down to the old cook house, and lay down before the fire, till the regiment was ready to start. I marched that night about eight miles, slept under a shelter tent. The next morning we started on a forced march. If it had not been that I made up my mind to keep up with the regiment, whether I could or not, I should have dropped out. When we got to Centerville I was a used-up man. I slept the first night in a shelter tent, and then went to the hospital, which was in an old-fashioned house. Here I got into a comfortable bed, and, with a bright fire burning on the hearth, it really seemed like home. I staid here only two nights, when the regiment again moved, this time to Bristow Station. I rode there in an ambulance; and Captain got his tent pitched, and we gathered some leaves to make a bed, and got fixed quite comfortable. Next night the Chaplain sent word to me to come over to his tent, and spend the night. I accepted his kind offer. He has a stove he is entitled to have carried. The regiment was ordered to be ready to march in the morning. When morning came, I concluded it best for me to try to keep with the regiment. I strapped my blankets that I usually carry on my back, and put them in with the baggage, as I did not feel able to carry them. I started on, but could not keep up. The regiment marched along the railroad, and I took the track. After I had gone two or three miles, I came by a soldier marching slowly. He said, if I was sick he had something for me. For I was about used up. This something, proved to be a canteen of whiskey," [which nothing but, extremity would have induced him to touch] "so I took a swallow or two, and got strength enough for another mile. After I had gone this distance, and was again about exhausted, I saw coming on behind me a hand car, pushed by four or five men from an other regiment, with cooking utensils. I asked them for a ride, and they took me on, as I told them I was sick and tired. After riding and getting a little rested, I offered to walk again; but they insisted that I should not. They went along at a lively gait, and we finally came up with our regiment. Here they stopped to rest, and I, pretty well rested, went on with the regiment. After marching with the regiment a mile or two, Doctor Collier offered me the privilege of riding his horse a little while. I rode a mile or so, and then we had not far to go. I got along pretty well. Of course, the baggage wagons did not come up, and my blankets were behind. The Doctor, however, got quarters for himself, several other men and me, in an old house with the windows knocked out, and the doors knocked in; but there was a good fireplace, and the Doctor gave me part of his blankets. I laid my feet to the fire and slept like a prince. The next morning we started back to Manasses Junction. I marched three or four miles, and then rode the Doctor's horse a mile or more, and then got into the ambulance, that had come on that morning, and rode the rest of the way, and slept again with the Chaplain. The Captain advised me to apply for leave of absence for a few days to go to Washington and get cured up. I concluded I would do so. The next day, I got the Doctor's certificate, the Captain's approval, and the Colonel's, and went to the Colonel commanding brigade. After waiting till five o'clock, he came in, and I got his signature. I thought I would see it through that night, so I started over to Gen. SICKLES' headquarters. His Adjutant General told me I would have to see Dr. SIMMS first, whose office was there, and that he would be in at nine o'clock in the morning. I then started back to camp, sick, disappointed and tired; it was so dark I could hardly see. I came along by a house that was occupied by a sick surgeon of our own brigade, so I asked the privilege of staying all night, which was cheerfully granted. He asked me to take supper, which I did, and slept on the floor, with my feet to the fire. I had my breakfast there the next morning, and then went back to see Dr. Simms; he told me there was a slight irregularity in the Surgeon's certificate; but that, if it was all correct, it would have to go, in the first place, to Gen. SICKLES, then to Gen.

HEINTZELMAN, commanding corps, and from there to Washington, before Gen. HALLECK, and that it would take at least ten days. I made up my mind to go back to the Chaplain's, and make myself as comfortable as I could; and I guess I have everything I need. I got through with my sick leave business yesterday and to-day. I feel very much better, and expect to be all right in two or three days. I do not lack for friends, and have everything I need. I will say this for the private soldier, whether in my own regiment or out of it, I never asked a favor of any single one that was not cheerfully granted; and I believe that ninety-nine of every hundred would give away his last hard tack. Now, don't be putting on the blues because I am sick, for I am getting better, and would not write until I could say, in truth, that I was better. I am all over the jaundice, but have had a very hard, tight cough, which is now growing loose; so that I begin to raise a little.

The prospect is, that we will not move very soon; so I shall have time enough to get well, which will not take long. The Chaplain is a first-rate man, and is kind to the sick; not only to officers, but privates; and to me he has been a good Samaritan. I have not time to write more, but will write in a few days again, if possible.

Affectionately, thy son,

E. H. KETCHAM."

CHAPTER IV.

ON THE MARCH.

THE brave spirit of EDWARD KETCHAM was more efficacious than medicine to restore his strength. The sense of duty absorbed his energies again, and we find his enthusiastic nature dictating the following manly letter to his mother :—

" MANASSES JUNCTION, Nov. 18th, 1862.

" DEAR MOTHER :

"I wrote home and said that I was sick ; but I am very happy to say that I am a great deal better ; in fact, about well. So don't feel uneasy, for nothing short of a rebel bullet will kill me, I think. We are now all the time expecting orders to march, to what place I do not pretend to know ; but the knowing ones say, to Fredericksburg, which, from every indication and the situation of our forces, I think not unlikely. I have seen nothing that leads me to think that we shall march to-day ; but we will not stay here long, as the railroad here is to be abandoned, because our army has got in such a position that they can draw supplies easier and better in some other way. They are getting the stores away as rapidly as possible, and when they are all gone, why then, of course, we will not be needed here to guard this road any longer, and we will probably then join our corps, that of Gen. Hooker's. Well, all I ask is health, and I am about well, and will be able to carry my blankets, and keep up with the regiment, without any trouble, and am worth now half a dozen dead men.   Once more, I have to urge thee to have no uneasiness about me, for I am not now sick, and if I were, I have never lacked for friends, and I don't think I shall; for, from the Colonel, all the way down to the private, I have asked no favors that have not been promptly granted.   I was just a little homesick for a day or two, while I was sick; but am over it now   I have faith that, when the war is ended, I shall be home again all right, and I only fear that I shall find thee the worse for the worry and anxiety that I know are bestowed on me.   Don't, for heaven's sake, fret and worry, on my account, if for no other reason; because I want to see my mother when I come back (if it is my fortune to do so,) as I left her, not broken down with useless anxiety on my account; so be as cheerful as possible, and think, if it should be my lot to be among those who are never to return, that I shall die doing my duty; and that is the way a man should die; for die he must, and a few years more or less don't make much difference, so that when the end comes it finds us at our posts with our harness on our backs.   It is not the business of a man's life to devote himself, simply, to saving that life; but to do his duty, whatever it may be, and let life take care of itself. So in either event don't feel uneasy about me, for I have no fear for myself, and I do not wish any one to worry uselessly for me. So, hurrah for the second grand army! It is going to do its duty, and it won't be sacrificed to strategy, thank God, with BURNSIDE and ABRAHAM LINCOLN.

Affectionately, thy son,

E. H. KETCHAM."

And again, to "Mother and Jack:"

"WOLF RUN, Nov. 23d, 1862.

"DEAR MOTHER AND JACK:

"I have now to tell that we have had part of our expected march, as I expected. I have been able to do duty all through it so far. We halted in the rain at Centreville, to get our dinner, which consisted of hard tack, a little piece of cooked beef or raw pork or bacon, and coffee. The coffee is generally cooked in a tin cup, with which each man goes armed; that was the way I cooked mine; and, after adding sugar, drank from the same cup. It really was excellent, upon that rainy day, sitting on the wet ground, eating a hard tack, and nibbling a piece of cold beef. It tasted as good as any coffee I ever drank made at home, where every convenience was at hand.

After we had finished our meal and rested a little, we moved on, the mud still getting worse and worse, until, in some places, we were literally, without any exaggeration, up to our ankles. We halted that night at Fairfax Church. It was dark when we stopped, having marched about twelve miles, pretty good marching under the circumstances. My tent was with the baggage train, half a mile off, in which direction, it was so dark, we could not tell. So I made my arrangements to get down under, or wrapped in, my blankets, with my rubber on, on the outside. One of the men offered to lie down in the rain and let me have his tent. Who would I be, to do that? But I crawled in with two men, where the third one had gone out on duty. So you see that, after all, there will always something turn up, no matter how dusty things may look. It did not rain quite all the time, and the boys made up a glorious big fire right in front of the tent; and whenever it did not rain, for a few minutes, I would dry my feet, and when it commenced again, would draw them in again. In this way, before I went to sleep, I had them thoroughly dry. My rubber blanket kept us from the wet ground, and my blankets, that had been wrapped in it, and were perfectly dry, kept me and one of the boys warm. So I slept on the wet ground, and kept dry and warm, wet over and wet under; but dry within the little shelter. I went through fire and did not get burned. I felt well in the morning, and the cough that had troubled me the night before, when I slept in a tent, with a fire and everything as comfortable as in a house, did not trouble me at all. · The next morning the drums beat for a start. I felt ready and better able to do a good day's marching than I did the day before."

At this camp, Lieut. KETCHAM remained some days, and then took up the march for Falmouth, from which place his next letter was written:

"FALMOUTH, Nov. 29th, 1862.

"DEAR MOTHER AND BROTHER:

"The last time I wrote to you we were at Wolf Run Ford. We arrived here yesterday, about two o'clock, and are now comfortably encamped, about (as the date of this shows) one-and-a-half miles from Fredericksburg, and our baggage-train came up last night.

The men were short of rations this morning, some of them being improvident, having wasted part of the two days' rations issued—and I be-lieve we did not receive quite full rations, either; but we expect the wagons up very soon now. Some had not enough for supper last night, and more than half of our company had nothing for break-fast; so I started out, this morning, on my own hook, and, after begging like a cripple, succeeded in buying ten pounds of crackers, or hard bread, which gave each man who had nothing a couple of crackers—rather a light breakfast, but better than none. For myself, I have had plenty, and some to give to others. This morning I was lucky enough to overhaul a rabbit that was going through the woods, close by camp, without taking the precaution to send out scouts, to see if the ground was occupied. He will make a good dinner, but if the men all around are hungry yet, he will not taste very good; but I guess the wagons will be here before that time. We started from our old camp, where we had lain three days, on the 25th, early in the morning, and marched about ten miles that day, crossing Wolf-Run early in the morning, fording the stream that came up to our knees. We were allowed time enough to take off our shoes and stockings, so it only amounted to washing our feet, which certainly did not hurt some of us. We encamped that night in a field that was soaked pretty well with water. I crawled into a tent, with three of the boys, and my rubber blanket compensated for the crowding I gave them. Although it rained some in the night, it amounted to nothing more serious than wetting the end of my blankets, that poked out of the tent, and made them a little heavy to carry. We did not march more than seven or eight miles the next day, the roads being so very heavy, and the division wagon-train being so constantly stuck in the mud, and in our way. I never saw such roads. Sometimes the wagons would sink down to the axle; it seemed to take a good deal of hard swearing to get them out. We encamped this night in a nice wood, along the road, which this day and the next ran all the way through pine timber—worn-out tobacco land, which had been abandoned, and grown up with pines. One of the boys, with whom I tented, was fortunate enough to knock over a good, fat turkey, that made a good breakfast for several of us, and left some to put in our haversacks. So I had turkey on Thanksgiving day, for breakfast and dinner.

We did not start very early the next morning, and moved slowly, on account of the bad roads and baggage-train, and halted an hour before sundown; but, just as the men had gathered wood, and part of them had their tents pitched, the order came to move on, and we had to pull up stakes, and jog along; much to the disgust of the men. We marched rapidly for about two or three miles, and then halted in a nice wood, when they soon forgot their anger in sleep. The next morning we moved on about six miles, to where I am now writing. We are now part of a grand army, and for the whole march yesterday, we passed encampments on each side of the road, and their name is "legion." Yes, we are now in the advance, and any hour we may be called upon to "up and at it." Some of the men and officers who have been talking, all along, about when we get into winter quarters, will probably find quarters that will last longer than the winter—longer than the war; and the plough, as it turns the sod fifty years hence, will turn out their bones, and the plowman will turn them over with his foot, with a "Killed at the battle of——." But it is not battles and bullets that kill the most men; it is exposure, improvidence, and hard marching. I cannot seem to realize that we are so near actual fighting, and, in fact, now think a good deal more about where our dinner is to come from, than about Stonewall Jackson. I want Jack to send me $25; not that my money is out yet, but I do not want to get out; I may sometimes want to spend a little for the boys, as I did this morning.

"Affectionately, your son and brother,

E. H. KETCHAM."

CHAPTER V.

A SOLDIER'S SPIRIT

FALLING back, from its position before the enemy, our army encamped near Falmouth; and from quarters there, Lieutenant Ketcham wrote letters to his home, filled with the manly confidence that was characteristic of his nature. One of these is dated—

"OLD CAMP NEAR FALMOUTH, DEC. 17th, 1862.
"DEAR MOTHER AND BROTHER:

"The last letter I wrote home, was dated "Field of Battle," and I supposed, from the preparations that were going on, that we were to have fighting in earnest; but at night, about eleven o'clock, we were waked up, and told to keep as quiet as possible; for the whole army were on the retreat across the river. We packed up our blankets, and got ready to start, and were then ordered to waken the men, as quietly as possible, and get them in line. Our division was then drawn up in line, in front of the enemy, to cover the retreat of the vast army. The men were not told what was up; but, with a constant passing of troops, mostly

on a double-quick, they knew as well as we, what
was up. Of all things to try the courage of new
troops, or old ones, is the position we then held;
with the cowards and stragglers, that had broken
away from their regiments, and were going on a
double-quick to the river, and calling out, " You
had better hurry up, or the rebels will have you."
But no man thought of leaving the ranks, until
our work was done, and we, too, were ordered to
the river. There was one regiment that had got
separated from its division, and came "skedaddling"
down by us, and going in all kinds of shapes;
while our men were in perfect order, almost. The
120th behaved like men, and I have no doubt of
our boys. The wind blew towards us from the
rebels, and we could hear them cutting wood for
their batteries—that is, clearing the timber—and
I don't believe they suspected our being off, till
hours after we were over. The thing was a perfect success; for moving such an army over a
narrow bridge, before the enemy, is a difficult
thing. I believe we could have whipped them
where we were, but it would have cost three of
our men to one of theirs; as we were on a plain,
commanded on every side, but the river, by a range
of hills, covered with timber, and planted with
batteries that would have been difficult for us to
get at. Gen. BURNSIDE knew his business; and
what has the appearance of a retreat, was really
a good piece of strategy; but I hate the word.
We did some skirmishing, and had the bullets

whistling close to our heads; and one night the rebels threw shells so close, that we could hear them "flop" in the mud. But enough of this fight. I am alive and well, and never felt better. I can sleep with or without blankets; with or without tent; with or without fire; with or without rain, in the middle of December; and come out next morning, lively as ever, and don't mind it.

I have never known what it was to really suffer, from hunger or cold; and I know that soldiers letters, (officers included) are, nine times out of nine, one-half exaggerations. So, don't believe the stories that will, doubtless, innocently and in good faith, be sent back to Milton, by the boys who came from there; for, in the eyes of some, a mole hill is a mountain. Don't think that, because I am an officer, I fare better than they. When it comes hard times in the field, there is no difference to speak of; only the men drew rations on the field, and the officers did not. I had bread and meat in my haversack, however, when I got back. We have got our tents and baggage, and are comfortable; and I have no trouble on my mind, except a fear that my mother may worry herself sick, on my account, though I hope she may not. Don't think I am going to be killed or wounded. It is all nonsense to borrow trouble from the future. I will live, if I am to live, and die if I am to die; which, I suppose, I shall some day—if not on the battle-field; and it is only a question of time. Next time we cross the Rappahannock, I guess it

will be a sure go; so, hurrah for BURNSIDE, and
our army!

      " Affectionately, your son, and brother,

                "E. W. KETCHAM."

In this manner, with his brave heart ever disposed to make the best of all situations, Lieutenant EDWARD KETCHUM kept his post of duty with
the regiment to which he belonged. His letters
to friends at home are all marked with the same
earnestness of purpose, and it was natural that their
effect upon his brother JOHN should be to stimu-
late a desire to follow so gallant an example.

CHAPTER VI.

"BROTHER JACK."

WHILE the elder brother was enduring, with cheerful spirit, the discomforts and fatigues inseparable from military life on the march, the younger one became daily more dissatisfied with his inaction at home. Every letter from camp was to him a fresh excitement. The desire to join his brother, and participate in the glories and dangers of their country's service, grew upon him constantly. It was his dream by night, his thought by day, to follow Edward to the battle-field. Affection for his mother withheld him, for many months, from declaring the wish of his heart; but, at length, he could no longer repress his feelings. The widow felt that her other boy was to be removed from her; that she must offer another sacrifice to the cause of her native land.

Then followed a pleading letter from "Jack" to Edward, disclosing his purpose to join the army, whether by enlistment or appointment, avowing his sense of duty, and his resolution to be guided by it. Edward was not prepared for this, and endeavored to dissuade his brother from the step

which the latter proposed to take. Zealous in the
cause of our Union as the young lieutenant was,
he could not but feel anxiety regarding a beloved
brother, and a mother, so dear to them, who must
be deprived of both her sons for years, and—the re-
flection was a solemn one—perhaps, forever. He
felt it to be an obligation upon him to combat the
wish that " Jack" expressed, by every proper argu-
ment ; and with this view he replied to him, in the
following letter :

" CAMP NEAR FALMOUTH, VA., Jan. 11th, 1863.
" DEAR JACK :

" I received a letter from you by Col. SHARPE,
and you may suppose I was somewhat surprised.
Now, Jack, if we were both at home, and each
knew as much as the other about the matter,
I would not presume to give advice ; but in the
present case, I " know" something about what you
purpose doing, and you do not. This should give
what I say some weight. I will state the case as
concisely as possible. You propose to come heref
and take. what place you can get. Jack, if you
should join the army, by right of education, intelligence and manhood, as well as by your habits of
life, you are fitted for an officer, and would make
as good a one as there is in the regiment ; but
it would be hard work to make men who have
been with us from the start, and who do not know
you, have that confidence in you that is essential
to make an officer useful, no matter how good he

may be. If you come, then, you will have to be a private or what is the same thing, a "Non. Com." Now, the chance of getting out of such a scrape by promotion is about equal to being struck by lightning. Jack! to men who have been used to obeying the will of others, the severe restraint of military law, when administered by the best of officers, comes tough enough ; but, when it is administered by a cowardly tyrant, as it often is, if the victim is a man who has pluck enough to do good service—and his habits have been such as yours have been,—he has pluck enough to get himself into trouble. Every man who holds a commission can protect his own rights; but though you may read the contrary in the Articles of War, as they are written on paper, I tell you I have read them written in another way; and as I have read them, a private or non-commissioned officer has no right, practically, that shoulder-straps are bound to respect. I tell you, you are too much of a man to be anybody's dog ; you have too much brains to be a simple cog in a great machine, and you can't be a crank. Now, Jack, I think I have as much patriotism as you, and am willing, if necessary, to die for the cause of the Unity entire of this government, and do not wish to live to see its overthrow ; but I am not willing to live a private. There is one other thing, the most important of all : our mother has a claim on you and me, equal to the claims of the nation. One of her sons is here fighting for his country. I have had a severe training and have a position where I am worth something—at least so I flatter myself. You have had no experience, and have no position where your worth can assert itself. The most ignorant man, or a jail-bird, would be worth in the ranks as much as you, perhaps more. I don't believe in using a shovel made of gold, to shovel mud, when one of steel would answer better. Our mother, in her declining years, has a right to one of her two sons, at least, and when I left home I thought that you would stay. You remember, when the war first broke out, that we cast lots, which should stay; it fell to you, and though it may come tough, stay like a man, and don't murmur. Jack! I·may fall a victim to rebel bullets, or disease, that strikes oftener and harder. I want you to stay at home, and save our name and race; for it is at least worth saving, and trust us, in spite of the disaster at Fredericksburg, to put it through and save the nation. We have changed camp to a lovely spot, and I have a comfortable shanty; about three feet by fourteen, and a good fire-place and chimney, and am as comfortable as you need wish to see a soldier; but it may be for one day, or it may be a month, no one can tell. I must close in time for the mail.

" Affectionately, your brother,

"EDWARD KETCHAM."

In a letter to his mother, a few days later, on the subject of his brother joining the army, he says :

" Understand me, I think no man too good to fight or die for his country ; but Jack can't take a place that is fitted for him in this regiment; because there is none open, and it is bad economy for a man with brains to take a place where he can only use his body ; besides, I cannot bear the idea of my mother alone and childless ; for she has the right to lean, in her declining years, on the strong arm of one of her sons ; a right that no duty to country can exceed ; but enough about Jack, he will do as he ought. If he can get a commission, let him come."

" CAMP NEAR FALMOUTH, VA., FEB. 18th, 1863.

" DEAR MOTHER:

" I received a letter from thee and John yesterday, and one from him to-day. I know, of course, it must come hard to thee to part with him, and be left alone ; but, still thee has kind and sympathizing friends, who will do all that they possibly can, to make thy hard lot, as I must call it, easy. Now, perhaps, it will somewhat soften thy grief, if I tell thee that the hardships of war are greatly exaggerated. I have seen men, who told awful stories of their sufferings in their campaign before Richmond, brought to admit, that what they were then enduring equaled any suffering they had before

met with.   Now, I have never yet seen the three
consecutive hours, when I suffered either from
cold, heat, thirst, or hunger ; or much on account
of fatigue,   Now, soldiers, as a rule, like to be
heroes ; in fact, that brought a large share of them
here, and if they don't exaggerate considerably, in
their letters home, why, their friends would not
have a chance to indulge in hero-worship ! Thus,
it comes, that wonderful stories are told ; and then
it is natural to make any transaction of their own
as big as possible, to some people ; so, the big
yarns find their way home. " Never believe but
half a traveler tells you," is a pretty safe rule ; but
when you come to a soldier, why, reject two-thirds
and trim the balance. Doubtless, the wounded
and sick have suffered ; but I believe that the
instances where the well soldier has suffered to
any great extent are scarce ; never from hunger ;
except, perhaps, when the baggage-trains have
been lost or captured.

But what if we do suffer some, occasionally, what
does it all amount to ?   Who expects to go through
life, gathering roses, from which the thorns have
been plucked ? The back should be shaped to the
burden. Mother, to tell the truth, I did cherish
a hope that Jack would be disappointed in getting
off ; but it seems I was disappointed. I hoped
this only on thy account ; for I believe these times,
and this war, call for just such men as he ; and,
though he is my only brother, and I know full
well his value, I would not have had him prove

himself not what I thought him, even if, by so doing, he had staid at home. I wish the necessity were not ; but, as it is, if he had chosen to stay at home, it would have gone far to prove that he was not worth coming. He may live to return a hero, or, he may die a martyr. But, in either event, he will have lived and done his duty, and he who, when death looks him in the face, can say, in truth, I have done my duty, has lived a lifetime, though the blood of youth still courses through his veins.

Lovingly, thy son,
EDWARD H. KETCHAM."

The kindly arguments of Edward Ketcham, to change his brother's purpose, were, as might be expected, of no avail; for "Jack" shared in the firmness characteristic of their family, and he had reasoned with himself long before finally adopting the resolution to become a soldier. To this brave youth, the same stern voice of duty that had invoked his elder brother was calling, with equal emphasis. If it was right in one to obey the summons, it must be wrong for the other to disregard it. The spirit of piety and patriotism combined to urge them both. They had alike sought counsel of their Heavenly Father, and the spirit had said to them, " Come !" Could the mere casting of lots absolve either from the necessity of obedience to that higher law of their nature which

declared their places to be in the front of battle ?
John's reason and religion said "nay" to this, and
he announced the verdict of conscience in his
reply to Edward's letter of the 11th of January.
In this rejoinder he says :

" I received yours of the 11th, last night. It is
all very good logic as far as it goes ; but if I had
gone to the war, and you were at home, you would
see it in a different light. You say, that, if you
knew that I would go, you would not have gone ; it
may be so, or it may only appear so to you now ;
but this I believe : you in my place would do as I
do. I know that it is mother that makes the
sacrifice. But in the grand result, this carnage,
and the hearts wrung with anguish, are as dust
in the balance. If this struggle goes against us,
and I at home, like a miserable clod-hopper, who
can't see outside of his own fences, the consciousness of not having done my duty would come
down upon me like the brand of Cain.

ED! I am thinking about the war, night and day,
and it is nonsense for me to try to keep out of
it. It is the place for a MAN, and, if there is any
man in me, MY place ; if not, no less.

I can arrange the business so as not to sacrifice
much. The most important thing is, the grief it
causes mother ; but I believe there is no grief of
that kind but has its compensation.

"JOHN."

CHAPTER VIII.

WORDS OF PATRIOTISM.

THIS tissue of cotton threads, which I fling out before me—what is it? No thrill of life responds from it; no voice returns my invocation of it; no pressure vibrates on my lips, as I enclasp and kiss it as a bride.

Yet for this web and woof of simple cotton, spun by hand or loom, there shall be myriads of men ready to lay down their lives, as myriads have done; there shall be tears and prayers, and kisses, and such deeds achieved for it as lift up mortals to be demi-gods.

For this tissue of threads, red, white, and blue, is the FLAG of my country. It is an emblem; it is a symbol; it is an imbodied idea.

Robing themselves in this drapery, men have wooed danger as a mistress, and died upon her bosom, exultingly. Wrapped in its starry folds, they have lapsed from suffering into martyrdom—from glory into immortality. Death-stricken heroes have looked their last upon it, and smiled as if mothers were blessing them. Fugitives from tyranny have caught its first gleams, with their souls leaping upward to worship it. The sick have stretched out their feeble arms to it; the

weary prisoner has yearned for its sight, as the
" hart panteth for the water brooks."

I have seen poor comrades in captivity creep
out of their huts, under the darkness of midnight,
and, clustering together like shadows, surround
this treasured emblem with their throbbing hearts,
and pass its precious folds from lip to lip, in
holy communion of patriotism.

Symbol of an idea—of manifold ideas—the flag
of an army, or a people, or a nationality, or a
cause—how immeasurable its influence—how ex-
alted its inspiration. Depress it, and the hearts
of men sink within them ; uplift it, and those hearts
become winged, like eagles. Its tissues are woven
into multitudinous memories—its colors are
blended with infinite hopes. There is no thread
of its web that is not moistened, no hue that is not
gilded, with the priceless blood of heroism.

Thus the flag becomes an emblem of faith, a
beacon of aspirations, a cynosure of veneration.
It writes, as with sunbeams upon ether, the name
and the path of a cause which it marshals. Yet
the flag itself is but a symbol. Its dazzle is but
the reflex of an idea that dwells in the army
or nation whose cause it foreruns and identifies.
That idea may be patriotism, or religion, or liberty ; whatsoever it be, it is the soul, whereof
armies and nations are but bodily manifestations.

And it is to some tender or gallant quality in
the man that a flag appeals so potently. I care
not if he be common soldier or sailor, or if his

shoulder be doubly or trebly starred; his soul must thrill lovingly to the waving of his flag, or he is no true man in the hour of trial. We have rank and titles, for leaders; princely guerdons for their services; monuments for their memories. But the IDEA of that cause, which upraised these heroes, may be far more vital in a private's soul than in that of his chiefest commander. The piety of a Christian is not measured by riches, nor restricted by poverty. The idea of patriotism or of liberty is not written upon a parchment commission, but upon the living heart of a man. Bright is the sword of a captain, but the flames of his powder-black muskets reach farther into the darkness of battle.

I follow, with hushed breath, the firm tread of a battle-line of unnoted heroes, or the double-quick of their charge into the bowels of fiery batteries. There is no waver in that foremost rank, no gap in all those files. Who, then, shall I choose out, as the hero-one? What matter is it that the few wear shoulder-straps and the many have no badge? There is no hero-one; they are all heroes. Captain, corporal, guide, or color-bearer, or drummer-boy; black-skinned or white; they are in one battle-line, and each man keeps his post in the march or the melee. Who, then, shall I choose as my hero? They are all heroes.

And such was EDWARD KETCHAM, in his single-hearted devotion to the flag and the cause of his country. This inspired him with courage in the

battle, as it upheld him with faith through rough
marches, and sustained him with hope, under pri-
vation and hardship. He bore himself upon the
field of Chancellorville, as a Christian soldier
should; and his noble reflections, committed to
paper after that sanguinary fight, are worthy of
being "learned and conned by rote," in every
household of our land. Brave youth! may his
words be prophetic as regards the good that is to
follow the evil of rebellion! That simple letter to
his mother, after the engagement at Chancellorville, is a memorial of her martyr son more honorable to his memory than the proudest eulogy
could be.

"CAMP NEAR FALMOUTH, MAY 12th, 1863.
"MY DEAR MOTHER:

· "I wrote to thee from the battle-field, after we
had come out of the fight, and telegraphed to thee:
and again after we had recrossed the river. If
thee received either, I, of course, do not know;
but I will repeat the vital part of both. Jack and
I are close together once more; both well and
hearty. This old camp was, during last winter, a
pleasant place. Winter has gone, and the quiet
and repose, that were then not only endurable but
somewhat pleasant, are so no longer; and I shall be
truly glad when we shall leave it, for good; I can
bid good bye to the old log cabin without regret.
Mother, the short campaign, which we have just
passed through, was one of hardship; but, to me,

its hardest experience was mere play; I am able to stand just such, for six months, without inconvenience. God help the army of the Potomac, if we are ever so hard-worked that I give out; for there are few that can stand the pressure after that. Mother, this time spent here is not lost time—I mean I personally sacrifice nothing. I have often thought that old age, that has no experience of hardship or adventure to fall back on, when the time comes that we live in the past as I now do in the future, must be somewhat barren. If I come out all right, and do not fail to do my duty, just the experience of the last nine months I would not part with for all the wealth of New York City.

It is commonly thought that a soldier's life is rather calculated to demoralize. I do not believe it. It may appear so on the surface; but there is many a man here in this army, who has never thought a serious thought before, who thinks now, and, when he goes back to home and friends, he will go back to realize that there is something for him to live for besides himself. IT DOES MEN GOOD TO SUFFER FOR A GOOD CAUSE. It somehow identifies them with it; and, as one good cause is linked with everything else that is good and noble, a man in fighting for liberty somehow fights his way to goodness. The general effect on the men here will be humanizing, and with peace—an honorable one as we mean to win—will come national virtue. It is a tough sight, for one who looks only on the surface, to see the noblest and the bravest of the land, limping, and bleeding, and dying, as I saw them on the field of battle. But, when you look upon a man who died stoutly doing his duty, and can realize that he died to save something better than life, it does not seem so awful as it would. It was an awful picture we looked upon the other day; but it had a bright as well as a dark side. There were many brave men who saw the last of earth, on that battle-field of Chancellorville, and many tears will flow, for many a year. But, what are these tears, to the bitter ones a mother sheds over an erring son, out of whom every thing good has died, and only his body lives. If we were whipped at Chancellorville, as the Copperheads say we were, I think such getting whipped, on our part, will soon use up the Confederacy. Their loss must have been fearful; for they came up, time after time, right in front of our batteries, closed en masse, and were just let to come close enough, when our guns, double-shotted with grape, would pile them in heaps, and send them back, utterly cut to pieces. This was not only one occurrence, but it was done over and over again. But I must stop.

Affectionately, thy son,

EDWARD H. KETCHAM."

CHAPTER VIII.

NOTES ON A MARCH.

FROM the notes made by EDWARD, on his march from Falmouth, a few extracts may here be interesting. The unstudied language of familiar correspondence affords a better insight to the thoughts and impressions of these youths than any labored rhetoric could give; and for this reason I have preferred to let their simple letters to a beloved parent portray the growth and progress of loyal sympathies, as well as depict the routine of camp experience. It was during the march which these notes of Edward Ketcham describe, that the brothers met for the last time on earth. Soon afterwards followed that terrible battle of Gettysburg, in which so many noble lives were offered up—sweet sacrifices to their country. On the march, the column to which our Quaker soldiers were attached, passed over Bull Run's storied ground.

"14TH.—— Fell in, and marched to Rappahannock Station; we then rested till daylight. At six o'clock we started and marched back to Mount Holly Church, near Kelley's Ford, on the very road we had come over the day before; met Jack there, and as we lay close together, I spent the day with him. Started at sundown, and marched all night, till seven in the morning, when we halted at Catlett's Station ; marching thence till we got to Rappahannock Station, over the same road which we had passed twice before.

15TH—— Halted at Catlett's Station, a distance of eighteen miles; lay there till two o'clock, when we marched to Manassas Junction, a distance of eleven miles ; making, in all we marched, thirty miles in about twenty-four hours. Here we encamped for the night, or rather bivouacked.

16TH.—— Lay still until the afternoon, when we moved half a mile, and pitched our tents. A day of rest put us in order for another march.

17TH.—— Started about ten o'clock, and marched about two miles, when we halted at Bull Run Creek, (below the bridge of the railroad, said to have been built by Beauregard, to take supplies to Centreville.) The bridge above the railroad was the scene of the chief fighting in '61. The trees are here marked occasionally by bullets and cannon balls. The valley, that the stream runs through, is one of the most beautiful I ever saw. The trees grow almost as luxuriously as in the tropics. One old fellow branches out into ten distinct limbs, a few feet above the ground ; any one of the ten might pass for a respectable tree. I, as well as half the army here, took a good bath ; we rested, and dined under the shade of those old trees, as large as giants ; a cool breeze was blowing at the time. It was hard to think that this beautiful valley was an historic one, because of the stream that runs through it once having been red with human blood. It is but a few days less than two years, since the battle of Bull Run was fought; and now, if I did not know it, I could pass through without seeing any thing to tell that it had ever been else than as peaceful as now. We crossed Bull Run at Blackburn's Ford.

18TH.—— Rested, and looked about us. Centreville is, or was, a nice little village of a dozen houses; it stands on a hill, and the country around reminds me of Chestnut Ridge, Dutchess Co.

19TH.—— Packed about ten o'clock, and started on the road towards Leesburg. We guarded the train of the 3d Corps. I had command of the company, and posted one man with every wagon, till the men were used up. We passed through a nice country, pretty well wooded. There was good evidence that troops had passed through; though the country had not been much disturbed.

20TH.--—— Lay still all day, near a house owned by a Delaware County man, who owns quite a nice place, and who fed us hungry Yankees in squads of fifteen or twenty; so much a head; a crowd of impatient men reaching back quite a distance. We are now at Gum Springs, about ten miles northeast from Centreville."

CHAPTER IX.

JOHN IN SERVICE.

From Falmouth our army moved on the march to intercept General Lee, the rebel commander-in-chief. At this time, the two brothers were serving in neighboring regiments, and their letters to the mother at home speak often of their mutual hopes and occasional meetings. Previous to marching, and while yet encamped near Falmouth, their head-quarters were separated only by the distance of half-a-mile; and the younger officer, in his cavalry camp, became soon initiated into the "ways and means" of a soldier in the field. One of John's earliest letters, after entering service, depicts his new surroundings, and displays the same high tone of feeling that is marked in Edward's writing. This epistle is dated :

"Camp near Falmouth, March 15th, 1863.

"Dear Mother

"I enclose this little scrap in Ed's letter. I found, to my surprise, when we arrived here, that Ed had been over here at our camp, looking for me. The two camps are next each other; about one-and-a-half miles apart. Ed is living here, as comfortably as most people do at home, with table, desk, arm-chair, bed, etc.; a smart boy to wait on him, and cook for him; a commissary within a few steps of his tent. Our place is improved some now; we have a nice fire-place built like a three-sided cob-house, and plastered with mud, a mortar bed of which we have convenient. We are camped in a beautiful piece of wood, "i. e." it was, before it was made for a camp; but considerably chewed up now. A road runs before our company street; the mud is just even with the tops of your boots when you step in it; six mules have to look sharp to get along with a light load; and on either side of the road the soil is as nice and dry as the "long pond" woods in summer. There is no discount on Virginia mud; it takes about a pint of water and a little mixing, to make a cart load of it, about like grafting wax. It is grand soil here; not a stone to be found in miles; very little swamp; nice hills and valleys; but all covered with pine forest; some splendid whitewood. This is bound to be a fine country yet; a splendid farming country, I have no doubt, very different from the bank of the Potomac west of Washington. We left Nehe (Captain Mann) in Washington, sick with measles. I have not heard from him since; but suppose he is all right, as he was getting better fast when I left him with a friend of ours, who told me afterwards, that he took him to Col. NICK SCHRAMS. He probably intends to stay till he is all right. I can hardly realize yet that I am with the grand army; it is like Yankee Doodle, who could not see the town,

there were so many houses. Get up on a hill,
though, and you see cities and towns and villages
of white tents on every hill-side. The army, I
should suppose, covers an area of fifty square miles,
so we cannot see much of it. I saw the flag
at general head-quarters, opposite Fredericksburg,
the other night, in a splendid sunset, from where I
stood ; the sun set just behind the flag ; somehow
I was reminded of Whittier's lines—

> " We wait, beneath the furnace blast,
> 　The pangs of transformation ;
> Not painlessly does God recast,
> 　And mould anew, the nation !"

although by what I could not tell, unless by
the lurid color of the sky, the black clouds, and
the old banner sailing so bravely on their background.

Good night, Mother ; take good care of thyself,
and be of good cheer. Aunt Sarah wrote me,
thee bears thy grief, as I knew thee would, and
does not sink down under it, as others, who did
not know thee as well as I do, thought thee would.
Keep good courage while the good fight lasts, and
I pray God to help thee, and to make me equal
to the work before me. Good night. Edward
wants to talk with me ; he says I am pretty good-
looking, but he gets tired of looking at me ; says
I can write more in my own tent.

Love to all,

JOHN."

CHAPTER X.

A GALLANT KINSMAN.

FROM that peaceful Ulster County village which gave our Quaker soldiers to the nation's cause, another noble volunteer went forth to fight his country's battles. This was NEHEMIAH HALLOCK MANN, a cousin of the two lieutenants, who entered the army from their neighborhood, and impelled by the same motives of patriotism that inspired the brothers. He became a captain of cavalry, serving under that daring leader, KILPATRICK, and was wounded dangerously in the battle of Aldie, in which fight the young cavalry general was for a brief space a prisoner in rebel hands. Mention is first made of Capt. Mann by Edward Ketcham, in a letter dated " Gum Springs," June 23d, 1863.

" We are still at this place ; I think we shall probably stay a day or two ; I have not yet heard from John since the fighting on the 17th ; but his regiment was engaged. There was more fighting on the day before yesterday. I have not yet heard if his regiment was in it. I know well, if he was, he did his duty, and hope he is all right. I tried mighty hard to get a paper yesterday ; but could not ; so, without knowing, I hope for the best,— which is certainly the best way. I expect Milton is now dressed in its garments of purple and green, the dress it wears in June : and among its green leaves and bright flowers, the young almost forget that, down here in Old Virginia, men are marching and fighting and dying, and thinking of home and friends.   But there are few that can think of the war without thinking of some friend tramping through the valleys and over the hills of old Virginia.   Pshaw! we don't need pity ; I am talking nonsense.   It is only the young and strong at home, who feel that this fight needs their help, while circumstances they cannot control keep them away, that are deserving of pity !"

Here the letter breaks suddenly, and a postscript is added :

"I have just seen Captain Mann, on his way to Washington.   He was wounded very seriously in the day before yesterday's fight.   Jack was not hurt in either fight.   The mail is just going.

Thy son,

EDWARD H. KETCHAM."

The above extract is the last of Edward's letters to his mother which has come into our possession. On the day upon which it was dated, his brother likewise wrote a letter home, wherein he gives the details of his cousin "Nehe's" gallantry in the action that nearly cost him his life.   Lieutenant John Ketcham belonged to the same regiment with Captain Mann, and the two cousins were closely attached to each other.

"GUM SPRINGS, June 23d, 1863.

'DEAR MOTHER:

"I have just seen Nehe, Captain Mann, off to Washington Hospital. I suppose, before this reaches thee, thee will have heard of the affair; for I telegraphed to Sarah, his sister, to join him there. He was charging, at the head of the regiment, just this side of Upperville, near the entrance of Ashby's Gap. After being driven back, the Captain called for the boys to follow him, and went in ahead himself. The boys followed, but not close enough to prevent his being engaged with about a dozen at him at once, he says. One fellow gave him a cut on his cheek, which knocked him from his horse; then, as he lay helpless on the ground, another shot him; the ball entering near the point of the left shoulder, and, cutting under the ribs, lodged in the muscles of the left breast. The doctors think he may recover; but I don't think it worth while to deny that his wounds are dangerous. He had just come out with the regiment, for the first time; having been in charge of a large dismounted camp. The night before the day of battle, his company were in high glee at his arrival. On the morning of the fight, I think he looked finer than I ever saw him—without exception, the finest soldier I have seen, with none of the brutality so common in the military character. I would give more for Captain Mann, commanding a brigade, than any general I have seen—

except, perhaps, KILLPATRICK, who frequently charges with the boys of our regiment. I have no doubt Captain Mann would command a brigade of cavalry, with the science he learned as an orderly, with as much ease and grace as if he had been accustomed to it for a lifetime. He was in command of a squadron that morning, and when we were ordered to charge a blockaded bridge, which a rebel colonel we captured told us they expected to hold all day, and the regiment stopped, under the fire of cannon and sharpshooters, behind walls and trees, horses and men dropping, and bullets whistling around—Captain Mann sat calmly on his horse, knowing the enemy were singling him out, until he got orders to dismount his squadron and clear the bridge, with the carbine. Then he took a carbine, and led the men over the bridge in three minutes. Such men as JOHN PAUL JONES and ETHAN ALLEN were made of the same stuff as he. His charge released Gen KILLPATRICK, who was taken prisoner through the fault of two regular regiments of cavalry. Three platoons of our squadron, Nehe's, Captain Hall's, and mine, were sent out in an open field, of fifty acres or so, facing a wood, in front of Upperville. We deployed as skirmishers, over half a mile, perhaps, and advanced towards the woods. When near there, a column of rebels charged on our centre, driving in the skirmishers—the single column followed by column in squadron front. Our forces advanced, the two regiments, and the rebels went back in the woods. When near the woods the regulars commenced charging across, in front of the woods; the rebs came out, formed, facing the flank. General KILLPATRICK rode towards the line, and tried to turn the regulars in that direction; but on they went, pell mell, until they all got by them—the rebs after them—and took KILLPATRICK. Keep hope and courage, mother, and all Nehe's dear friends. His voice will soon be heard where it is needed—on the field of battle. Be of good cheer, high hope, and courage always.

Lovingly,

JOHN."

CHAPTER XI.

GETTYSBURG.

FROM the radiance of crimson sunsets we drink
assurance of golden morrows. So, dwelling upon
the battle-glories of America, I recognize in their
bright reflex the promise of lofty destiny. Great
deeds are prophecies as well as achievements.

Thus, in recalling heroic examples, we ascend, it
seems, some breezy height, wherefrom we look out
clearly to a future of kindred heroism. Going
back to that day of April, when the blood of Revolutionary Massachusetts was sprinkled over her
primroses, in fields about Lexington and Concord,
I gaze forward to that other day of April, when
blood of Massachusetts moistened the streets of
Baltimore. The Yorktown of our first struggle
presaged the Yorktown of our second one. The
cannon of Sullivan Island, in 1776, gave voice to a
principle that was to be thundered from multitudinous cannon-throats eighty-eight years thereafter. Moultrie and Marion uttered the first protest against Despotism in the Carolinas ; and that
protest, never resting, must needs recoil upon
Slavery in the Carolinas. Virginia blazoned upon
her shield the judgment of tyranny ; and that
judgment became her own most righteous con-

demnation in the last great struggle for Freedom.

Therefore it is, that the grand epochs of our national story are like the columns that were reared upon the route of an ancient army, inscribed with the names of its leaders and the exploits of its arms. They survive, not only as records of victory, but as guide-marks of following marches. The shaft that our present generation erected upon Bunker Hill is not the real pillar of guidance to coming democracies; it is but a material land-mark. There is a higher column, built of the deeds and crowned with the hopes of Bunker Hill, which becomes the true beacon of future republicanism. To this shaft, and to like monuments, wherever they arise, the eyes of watchful and waiting patriots in every land look out from the shadows that oppress them. To these yearning souls, our Republic's march is fraught with solemn significance. To them our memorials of Liberty have deeper import than to us. They crouch in the darkness, while we stride out under the light. They behold our nation's progress, through all the years, as a captive discerns, beyond his dungeon-bars, the procession of a conqueror, ascending broad causeways and outspreading upon limitless plains, "terrible as an army with banners." Thus evermore, to the waiting and weeping peoples, our American Republic presents a spectacle sublime and inspiring.

Thus the battles and conflicts of our Past were but initials of a national lesson; the opening-blows of pioneers, blasting a path for us. One victory over wrong gives earnest of greater victories that are to come, and must come, though many interposing defeats shall retard their advent. God's purposes cannot retrogress. Once declared, they become immortal, like their Author, and eternal, like His power. A good cause can await its day of triumph.

Infidels to the faith of humanity are those who distrust the future of free principles. Such men shook their heads oftentimes during our conflict with Rebellion. Such men doubt Omnipotence.

But DOUBT never entered into the minds of our loyal Quaker soldiers, whose gallant service is modestly recited in their own simple letters to a worthy parent. That portion which records the thoughts and feelings of EDWARD KETCHAM is finished. His mission was earliest accomplished, by a brave death upon the field of GETTYSBURG; and we turn to the letters of his surviving brother for an affecting account of the circumstances.

The story of Gettysburg, in all its details, will be a lasting memorial of courage and devotion. That battle was the turning-point of our national fortunes. The deeds of our officers and the glorious rank and file who supported them will live in the history of our Republic, and their results endure as the heritage of a restored Union. The names of Gettysburg's heroes and martyrs—an illustrious roll of patriots—will be inscribed on monuments; their stories will enlist the pen of

future chroniclers; their examples will inspire the
hearts of our citizens.   And among them all the
names of our "Fighting Quakers" will claim ap-
propriate honor.

The following letter is from JOHN KETCHAM, describing his brother's death:

"FREDERICK CITY, JULY 8th, 1863.

"DEAR MOTHER :

I telegraphed to thee as soon as I could, and
wrote about Edward.   I cannot realize that he is
dead.   Don't let it kill thee, mother!   Thee and
I are all that is left of us.   Edward was the first
man killed in the regiment.   They were lying on
the ground, behind a little mill, in front of our batteries, making a part of the outer line of battle.
It is always necessary in such times for some one
to keep a lookout, to watch the movements of the
enemy.   As the men all lay on their faces, Edward
was sitting up to look; a sharpshooter's bullet
probably struck him in the temple, and went
through his head.   He put up his hand, and said :
"Oh!" and fell on his elbow, quite dead.   There
was heavy fighting on the ground soon after, and
our forces had possession of the field for a short
time.   Ed's body was carried back a couple of
hundred yards, and left under a tree.   I heard of
it the next morning, and went to the regiment,
and got a man to go with me, who helped to carry
him off; he showed me where he lay.   It was

outside of our breastworks forty or fifty yards, and a couple of hundred beyond our outer line of sharpshooters. I went out to them, but could not get beyond; for a bullet would whistle by, the moment a man showed himself. I lay down behind a big rock. The body of Green Carle, of the 120th, lay there, horribly mutilated. They said he had lived two or three hours after he was struck. Whilst I lay there, two rebel batteries commenced to play on ours. I never imagined such a thunder as the firing made; there were twenty-four cannon at work, and the shells burst over our heads, fifty feet or more; one or two men were hurt near me, and the limbs of the trees dropped occasionally. I then took a musket, thinking I would stay with the infantry, till they advanced, as I was not needed with the department, it being with the mule train; the rest of our regiment was at Washington. Pretty soon the rebels came out from their works, in heavy force, and advanced in line. Our batteries commenced to mow them down, and the men lay down until in close range; then the outer line raised up, and the two lines fought, without either moving from their place. It was a grand, but terrible sight! The rebels concentrated on one part of our line, and pressed it back, to charge our breastworks; our flanks closed in on them, and hundreds were driven in, prisoners, while the rest ran back to their lines like sheep. One poor fellow came in just by me; the first words he said

were, " Gentlemen, I do this because I am forced
to." He was a pleasant, harmless-looking fellow,
as are one half of them; the other half look like
wild beasts. At this time, the 120th came up, and
I went with them. I went out at night, to look
for Edward, but could not find him. The next
morning our line advanced, and I went out to the
tree; and there, on his back, his hands peacefully
on his breast, lay all that was left of the brother
I have lived so closely with, all my life. When I
had been separated from him a few weeks, I have
known when I met him, how closely I was knit to
him. On this earth I will never meet him again!
His features, though discolored and swollen, had
an expression I have seen on them before—peaceful rest. He had lain thirty-six hours on the field,
with the roaring of cannon and bursting of shells
over him, and the feet of contending hosts, of darkness and freedom, trampling the ground he lay on.
When I got him, I brought him in through the
batteries, and laid him down under a tree. A
Captain of one of the batteries said to me, " If he
were a brother of mine, I would bury him on the
field of his glory." He was very kind, and sent
me men to dig the grave. In a little grove behind
the batteries, under an oak tree, in his soldier's
uniform, wrapped in a shelter-tent, lies all the
earthly remains of my brother; "he has gone to be
a soldier in the army of the Lord." And mother,
thee and I walk this world of sorrow. I set for
his head-stone a piece of a young oak, cut off by

a rebel shell, and marked his name and regiment.
Mother, yet a little time thee and I have to walk
this earth, when we compare it to the great eter-
nity beyond, where father and Edward are gone
before us.

Oh, he was cut down in the very morning of
his manhood! He is laid a sacrifice on the altar
of Liberty!

He died to give to every other man the right to
his own manhood—a precious sacrifice—for in him
were heroism, a brave heart, and an iron will. He
died, as he would have died—with his face toward
the enemies of freedom, on the battle-field. Edward has marched many a weary mile; he has
lain on the wet, cold ground, with nothing over
him, long nights, with the rain pouring on him,
and never murmured; he has lain and shivered
in the snow and slush, all long winter nights,
after weary marches, hungry, perhaps, or after
eating a few hard crackers, and a little raw meat;
and, in his discomfort, he has never wished for
home; except, perhaps, to look forward to that
bright day when the rebellion should be crushed,
and he should return home, war-worn, and covered
with his well worn honors. That day, alas! he
can never see. Oh, God! Thy price for freedom
is a DEAR ONE!

JOHN."

CHAPTER XII.

INFLUENCE OF PATRIOTISM.

THUS "marching on," the two lieutenants drew, one by one, to the holy altar of sacrifice. Each was a portion of that "grand army" of loyal souls whose bodies were destined to sink by the way-side; but whose luminous examples are to light the path for innumerable armies in the great future. Both were to be called from their brief career to an enrollment in those immortal ranks whereof all champions and saviours of humanity in the Past are the advanced guard, and to which have been transferred from gory graves such multi-tudes of heroes in the Present.

All the inspiration that history or tradition can give, is reserved for the warriors of Freedom. Monarchs and conquerors of old may be rever-enced by their descendants or their imitators; but the people have no sympathy for them; the peo-ple surround not their altars. It is the TELL of Switzerland, the WALLACE of Scotland, the WASHINGTON of America, the GARIBALDI of Italy, that lay hold of the popular heart with grapnels of love and authority. Liberty is rich in her jewels, of heroes who lived and of martyrs who perished for her. Scaffold and block have been consecra--

ted by the blood of her confessors and champions. The South is full of lowly graves, where the dust of those who died for freedom and equality shall bloom forever, with priceless balm, that will some day bear " healing for the nation."

But the defender of an unjust cause can leave no memory. For the dead traitor there is no resurrection in the hearts of his countrymen. Courage may have distinguished him ; endurance, even in the wrong, may have marked him ; a warrior's death may have expiated his errors ; but there is no sweet savor of patriotism to embalm him ; and the immortality of Liberty's children can never—oh, never—be his ! It is mercy to his name that it perishes from remembrance, and a boon to his posterity that no stone records it.

There was an old man of Gettysburg, whose musket was shouldered in the war of 1812; whose head was white with the snows of seventy years ; and when he saw the base flag of Disunion blotting the sunshine of his cottage door, he took down an old State musket from the wall, moulded a score of bullets, as in the times of old, and made ready to defend his homestead. Anon came the Stars and Stripes through Cumberland Valley, and the gray-haired veteran presented himself to our soldiers.

" Take me with you," says the man of seventy years. " I can still peer over a rifle-sight."

And they took him with them—those brave Wisconsin boys to whom he showed himself ; and that true-hearted old soldier fought in the ranks at Gettysburg, and was left, with three wounds, upon the field, within sight, almost, of his hearth-stone. God be thanked that the ancient hero survived our dread conflict, and that he dwells in peace at this day in his cottage by the battle-ground of Gettysburg. Worthy to bear the name of BURNS—the name of a free-souled poet—was this old fighter for the Republic. Poor though this brave JOHN BURNS may be, he will bequeath to his children a heritage of honor that no Lee nor Beauregard, with all their chivalry, have now in their bestowal.

In the days to come, our heroes of rank and file will be held in tradition as we now hold the " Liberty Boys," and the men of " Marion the Swamp Fox." Ballads will chronicle their fights " hand-to-hand," and their " hair-breadth 'scapes i' the imminent deadly breach" of siege and sortie. It is of their example that our future nation will eat and drink, to become robust in patriotism. " God keep their memory green !

There is always an influence of good emanating from the lives and deaths of our soldier-patriots. " A man in fighting for liberty somehow fights his way to goodness," said EDWARD KETCHAM. If he earnestly FEELS his share in such a fight, it ennobles him, I think. If he survives, it will be to exert a power for good on others. If he dies, his brave example will not die. It cannot die. It is immortal.

So, in the record of our war for Union and Freedom, its incidents of personal valor and devotion,
that are cherished permanently, will be as lessons
of patriotism to the generations that shall follow
our own.   Soldiers, in future days, will remember
that bold Sergeant BRUNER, of the Twenty-third
Wisconsin volunteers, in the fight at Port Gibson,
where he caught the colors from their disabled
bearer, and planted them on the ramparts, amid
a storm of bullets.   And again, at Champion Hill,
where he seized the flag, as our line was breaking,
and, crying out—"Boys, follow ! Don't flinch from
your duty !" led the regiment into order and victory.   And once more, at the battle of Big Black,
under the eye of GRANT, when the valiant Sergeant
led his men against a battery which had dismounted one of our cannon and dispersed its support-
ers,—twice in the melee was bold Bruner made
a prisoner by the foe, and twice his comrades res-
cued him.   And he brought to Gen. GRANT the
last one of three rebel flags captured by his own
hand from the enemy.   It is in the hearts of such
men as this that the IDEA of a cause is enshrined,
like a jewel in its golden casket.

And that old man-of-war's man, WILLIAM REID,
in his fiftieth year, one of the noble sailors whose
bravery almost redeemed the treachery of their
flag-captain at Galveston ; I can see him, in my
mind's eye, as he stood on the Owasco's deck, with
his left hand well nigh shot away, and a shot-
wound in his shoulder, where the blood oozed

through his shirt, while, holding still a rifle in his grasp, he fired upon the enemy. "Go below, and get your wounds dressed," said the master's mate. "No, sir," the veteran cried; "so long as there is fighting to be done, I'll stay on deck!"

What patient courage—what noble self-devotion—is common to the sailor at his gun and the soldier in his ranks; so common, indeed, that no note is made of it; so habitual, that it is looked upon but as the mere routine of duty. Assuredly, there is a motive-power deeper than mere routine to inspire these unrecorded heroes of our nation. Was there not true nobility in that common seaman, SAMUEL WOODS, who, fighting at his gun, with resolute courage, yet found heart to plunge into the stream, to save a shipmate who had been borne overboard, and then, returning, knelt beside his wounded comrades, nursing them like a tender woman, as he had fought with them, like a hero-man. Was there not cool and provident valor in that cockswain of the Wabash, EDWARD RINGGOLD, who, in service with the howitzer corps, performed his duty with such faithfulness, and, hearing that the powder had run low, passed up through all that fiery line, with his "shirt slung over his shoulders and filled with ammunition, which he had brought two miles from the rear!" Well did these men deserve the medal they won for "gallantry in action."

The examples and influence of such as these will blossom over their last resting-places, however

lowly they may lie. ` They will always make fra-
grant the cause of Union and Freedom. And this
simple memorial of our Quaker soldiers, which
goes forth to seek a household welcome wherever
patriotism dwells ; these unpretending letters of
two good brothers to their 'mother, may yet be
powerful, in their sphere, to strengthen the love of
liberty and of our native land.

We now draw near the end, with John's last
letters to his bereaved mother :

" NEAR SHARPSBURG, JULY 12th, 1863.
" DEAR MOTHER,

" I suppose thee has read either one or the other
of my four letters, and the telegram about Edward.
Keep heart and courage,mother ; he has only gone
beyond us. It is a comfort to think, that his
suffering was so short. He must have been con-
scious an instant, for he spoke in his natural voice
and said "Oh !" (not an involuntary groan) put his
hand to his forehead and fell on his elbow dead.
One instant of terrible pain, and the life which he
loved, as all strong men do, faded from his sense,
and was changed for the great Hereafter, when all
human imperfection is changed for perfection.
Brother ! our paths through life have run side by
side, diverging, but to join again. Now, you have
the better part, above the petty strifes of this life. `
All that is noble and glorious is yours, while I
must mingle with earthly scenes, till your life
fades into memory, and perhaps memory fades

into shadow. Surely, God in his mercy cannot let the life we have lived together be no more ; but in the great Hereafter, the life that has been shall live again in memory, fresh as the present. Edward ! your love for me was strong, strong for your younger brother, as your own great, strong, brave heart, and I have taken it as I do the sunshine, and thought to have you by me always ; but we are divided now. I am yet of the earth, while your name is on the long roll of honor— one of those whom God has considered worthy to be sacrificed. You were cut down in the morning of manhood, strong and brave heart. You never flinched from danger. I know, in your great love for me, you will be with me if I go in danger, and inspire me with your spirit, that I may do my whole duty without flinching and without fear. In the morning of life, your blood has been shed for the right of every man to upright manhood—that the poor slave-mother may hold her child to her bosom without fear of the driver. My poor, broken, widowed mother has given her first and noblest son. Oh, God have mercy on her ! Thou, " who doest all things well." Your body rests on the field of glory. Your name is on that roll of the noble dead to which posterity must bow down, and thank in reverence.

Napoleon told his soldiers, at the Pyramids, Centuries look down from the tops of these Pyramids. Forty centuries look down upon you ! Yes ! but, from the mountain over your head, the thunder of our cannon, hurling death to the rebels before you—from the top of that mountain, overlooking the field of Gettysburg—our great free nation, (yet to be,) looked down and saw you when you fell, and will hold your name in grateful honor, for all time to come!—better than the golden letter Napoleon wrote to immortalize his victims. You are one of the noblest dead who died for Freedom, and the feet of freemen shall tread the soil you fell on, for all time to come. A little mound, on the battle-field, covers all that is left of my brother, a noble fellow as ever drew the breath of life. As Christ "died to make men holy," he has "died to make men free." Have his picture, in his soldier's uniform, copied like thine and father's, and, under the glass, fold his commission and the ragged shoulder-strap I cut from him; hang under it his broken sword, and write:

"A SOLDIER IN THE ARMY OF THE LORD."

Now, I pray the battle soon to be fought may be decisive, and that I may return to be a little comfort to thee.

JOHN."

And so the elder died. And the younger was spared but a little longer, to write his last loving words to the poor, bereaved mother, and to pay a manly tribute to his gallant comrades of our army.

" HARPER'S FERRY, July 18th, 1863.
" DEAR MOTHER,

"I have heard nothing from thee since Edward's death, until two days ago. I had a letter from Nehe, and then, July 8th, you had heard he was wounded. I do not know hardly whether to suppose thee is alive or not. My comfort is, that Edward died as becomes a man, his face towards the enemies of freedom. I know that, though he loved his life as dearly as any man, yet, had he foreseen the result when he first thought of going to the war, it would not have made a particle of difference with him ; but he would have walked to certain death without flinching. I can do or say nothing to comfort my poor stricken mother. In thy boundless love for thy children, thy bereavement is more than mine, lonely and sad as I am, " wretch even now, life's journey just begun."

Harper's Ferry! How much, since the great page of this people's life-history was opened, is here. That long old row of blackened walls was the Arsenal, from which John Brown thundered out the challenge to a life and death struggle. Retribution visited upon the oppressor ; sacrifice of the best and noblest to atone for our wrongs upon the helpless ; lines of earthworks, overlooking Maryland heights ; white tents, houses battered by shot and shell into heaps of ruins, in the field where I am sitting ; pontoons across the river ; and the old battered and worn-out army, thinned out to one-fourth of the men who first buckled on the knapsack, crossing again into Virginia, to grapple with its old enemy, to lay the bones of its best and bravest before the breastworks and rifle-pits of the yet formidable rebels!—all the long story of weary suffering, and the woe of five hundred battles! and here we stand as evenly-matched as ever, and they on chosen ground, as ever. I don't overlook the great blows struck by GRANT at Vicksburg, and perhaps others, before this, at Charleston, which lead to the hope, almost, that the great price is nearly paid, and the work nearly done. I wrote thee I would resign if events occurred that showed the war nearly over; but surely thee would not have me back out from this glorious struggle, while the chances hang in the balance. Go home! and leave these weary war-worn men to fight for blessings I should enjoy? these weary men, who have fought and suffered so hard and long, addicted to every vice, almost, individually, but cowardice or meanness. I have seen them struggle, through mud and rain, after the defeat at Chancellorville, back to the cheerless ruins of their old camps. I have seen them making long and weary marches along the dusty road, to foil the advance of Lee across the Rappahanock, then, forced marches to Manasses, all day long without water; then, I have seen long columns pushing forward, with tireless energy, to meet the enemy at Gettysburg; then, marching, day and night, to cut off the retreating foe, and now coming here, to this old historic spot, down again into the dark valley and shadow of death, never halting or murmuring, ever ready to lay down their lives, as their comrades have done. I have heard them groaning in agony, wounded, jolted over rough road, or carried by their comrades, or lying on the battle field, between the lines, begging to be taken out of more danger. I have seen mangled and torn masses knocked out of the shape of men. I have seen ragged uniforms of United States soldiers, bursting from the black and swollen bodies, as they lay in ditches by the road side, rotting in the sun. "Blessed are they that endure to the end." I am no such soldier as my brother was; but I trust I have manhood enough to stand with this army of the Lord until its victory is sure. I entered the vineyard but at the eleventh hour. I can, perhaps, do but little, but, while the result hangs in the balance, I know, in thy heart of hearts, thee is glad that I am one of this army, and where is heard the tramp of their marching feet, there am I. I am glad to hear, from thy letter, that cousins V. Hallock and T. Sherman have gone for Edward's body. I know it would have been his wish; it is but a small satisfaction, but I could not have done even that. Bear up a little longer, my poor bereaved mother.

Thy only son,

JOHN."

CHAPTER XIII.

THE PRISONER OF WAR.

AFTER the death of his brother, JOHN KETCHAM continued in service, attached to his regiment, the Fourth New York Cavalry. His letter, closing the last chapter, portrays the high principle which prompted him to this course, although every feeling of affection called him to the home where a widowed mother sat weeping for her first-born. Edward Ketcham had been deemed the stronger-souled and self-reliant brother; but in the bosom of John a sense of duty was as inflexible and powerful. He felt himself constrained to keep the post which he had taken. His brother had fallen in the defence of his country. It was not for him to turn back from the glorious example set by that devoted brother. He loved his mother; but he loved Liberty likewise; and Liberty had summoned him to her banners. In good time he hoped, under the mercy of God, to return and comfort the bereaved one; but " where the tramp of our army's marching feet" was heard, there he elected to be, until the triumph of that army should no longer " hang in the balance."

But the hope of being a " comfort to his mother" was never to be realized by our young soldier.

The fatigues of incessant marching, the exposure to all vicissitudes of season; the constant recollection of his lost brother, with whose existence his own had been entwined, were slowly undermining the manly strength and gallant spirit which he brought to the service of his country. Day by day he grew less able to endure the exposures inseparable from duty during an active campaign, and at length, in the latter part of July, he reluctantly reported for the sick list, and was sent to the Seminary Hospital, at Georgetown, D. C. Here he remained four weeks, and should have rested longer. Here he was nursed tenderly by his mother, who had hastened from her home to attend him; and here he parted from her embraces, never to return to them in life. Sad was the separation; ominous the farewell. The afflicted mother returned to her lonely cottage; the son, already marked for sacrifice, rejoined his regiment at the front.

Three weeks afterwards, in an engagement with superior numbers, Lieutenant John Ketcham was captured by the enemy, and carried to the rebel capital, a prisoner-of-war. He was in no condition to report for duty when he left the hospital; but his anxiety to do so imparted temporary strength which was unequal to the constant hardships borne by our cavalry at that period. When to these hardships succeeded the rigors of rebel captivity, it might have been easy to foretell the consequences. Lieutenant Ketcham was to add one more to the thousands of Union soldiers whose souls fled from their tortured frames in the dismal prisons of the South. His spirit was to mingle with that host of martyrs, whose lives were not forfeited in battle, but by the slow torments of disease and famine.

The records of our grand struggle for Union and Freedom—so rich with the action and achievement of noble citizens—are not complete without those dismal pages that chronicle captivity and suffering. The horrors of Southern stockades and dungeons, in which our noble soldiers, held as war-prisoners, were treated as malefactors, must fill up the dark background of the picture that delineates a nation's triumph. History will have more to dwell upon than battles and marches; more violence to deplore than the bombardment of forts and the sack of cities; more cruel deeds to narrate than the slaughter of armed men in battle, or the firing of homes in a ravaging expedition.

For, in our terrible strife, we were contending with a power more inhuman and sanguinary than that of mere war—fierce and unscrupulous as war always is. We had pitted against us a demoniac spirit which has been known in all ages as Oppression; that spirit which manifests itself in the form of human slavery, and which is so brutalizing in its influence that it can change a woman into a fiend, and a child into an imp of cruelty.

By the hardening contact of this spirit of Oppression or Slavery, the natures of a large portion of our adversaries had been already indurated against tender sympathies, when the blast of intestine strife added intensity to their hate and fury to their passions. The wretched negro, so long a footstool for pride, became at last the instrument of its punishment. Treason and Rebellion had conspired to build a new temple to Moloch, whose walls were to be cemented by the blood of a free nation, and whose corner-stone was to be Human Slavery! Such were the calculations of the men who precipitated Secession, inspired by the arrogance which sprang from ownership in a servile race. But the Most High had ordained that their schemes should be confounded through the very means which they chose to accomplish them. To consolidate Slavery, they had invoked War. By War the power of Slavery was to be overthrown, and its victims relieved from their thraldom. Only through throes of violence and disruption could the new birth of Freedom be secured to our Republic.

It was a long time before even a glimpse of the inevitable fate that awaited them could be admitted to Slavery's advocates. I doubt if all have yet recognized the doom pronounced upon their unholy cause. To many at the South the idea of Liberty itself was strangely associated with that of African servitude. Multitudes were ignorant enthusiasts in the defence of what they deemed their Independence. The most sacred rights of "property" were involved in their estimation with the claim, which they deemed just, of ownership in negro labor.   Other multitudes, who were destitute of property in slaves, were yet champions of an institution which degraded the very industry whereby they sought to live.   Strange anomalies of motive were fused into fanatical cohesion with common bonds of Southern birth and citizenship.   But it was the belief in Slavery that constituted the touchstone of Southern patriotism everywhere.   It was property in, and superiority over, the negro race that formed a "Shibboleth," by which the true Secessionist was always recognized.   That was the stimulus to strife, the object of fighting, the stake of fortune.   It animated alike the regular and the guerilla; it prompted the assault on Fort Sumter, not less than the massacre at Fort Pillow.   It was the motive that lay at the core of Quantrell's outrages in Kansas, as well as the crimes of Winder and Wirz at Andersonville.   Had the spirit of Slavery been wanting, our civil war would have been conducted at all times according to the laws of war and of nations.   But Slavery interposed with its fiendishness; and the result was that book of murder whose livid leaves are rebel war-prisons, and whose letters are the epitaphs of unnumbered loyal victims.

It was to the "tender mercies" of this fell spirit of Slavery that unfortunate Unionists were consigned by rebel authorities.   In other lands, among people claiming to be civilized, and in this age of Christian liberality, a prisoner-of-war possesses rights which are held sacred as those of soldiers. Once captured, and delivering up his arms, he is no longer considered as a belligerent, to be feared or maltreated, but as a military hostage, for whose safety and good treatment his captors are responsible to the government which claims his service. But, in the usage of our late adversaries, the claims of a prisoner-of-war were ignored or derided. Practically, a "Federal prisoner" had no rights which a "Confederate" was bound to respect. Hated as a foe, abused as a criminal, preyed upon as spoil, and subjected to wanton outrage, the hapless United States soldier who fell into rebel hands seemed cast at once beyond the pale of civilization. Immured in loathsome jails, crowded in pestiferous hospitals, packed in filthy stockades; exposed to wintry cold and summer heat, without shelter; abandoned to thirst and starvation; robbed and stripped; encompassed by foul miasms; tortured with horrid punishments; shot at in sport; assassinated in malice; driven to madness and suicide; such were the consequences of capture to our brave soldiers and sailors, that the fortune of war rendered powerless to resist or escape.

It was in "Libby Prison" that Lieutenant John Ketcham was confined; an abode of wretchedness which has been graphically described by more than one poor inmate of its walls.

A three-storied stack of brick buildings, former-

ly used as a tobacco-warehouse, and overlooking
the Canal and James river—its rooms one hundred
feet long by forty feet in width—this was the now
historic Libby Prison. In six of the rooms, at
one time, twelve hundred United States officers,
from the rank of brigadier-general to that of
second lieutenant, were incarcerated, and treated
as convicts instead of soldiers. Ten feet by two
was the average space of floor allowed each man,
but little more than the dimensions of a grave ;
and in this limit they were constrained to sleep,
work, cook, eat, and exercise.

"At one time," says a report to the Sanitary
Commission " they were not allowed the use of
benches, chairs, or stools, nor even to fold their
blankets and sit upon them ; but those who would
rest were obliged to huddle on their haunches, as
one of them expresses it, ' like so many slaves on
the middle passage.'

"They were overrun with vermin, in spite of
every precaution and constant ablutions. Their
blankets, which averaged one to a man, and
sometimes less, had not been issued by the rebels,
but had been procured in many ways ; sometimes
by purchase, sometimes through the Sanitary
Commission. The prisoners had to help themselves from the refuse accumulation of these
articles, which, having seen similar service before,
were often ragged and full of vermin. In these
they wrapped themselves at night, and lay down
on the hard plank floor, in close and stifling con-

tact, crammed and dovetailed together, as one of them testified, "like fish in a basket." The floors were recklessly washed, late in the afternoon, and were therefore damp and dangerous to sleep upon. Almost every one had a cough in consequence. There were seventy-five windows in these rooms, all more or less broken, and in winter the cold was intense. Two stoves in a room, with two or three armfuls of wood to each, did not prove sufficient, under this exposure, to keep them warm."

From the statements of prisoners, who passed months in this lazar-house, it appears that " the hideous discomfort was never lessened by any renovation in the cells, but often increased. The prison did not seem to be under any general and uniform army regulation, but the captives were subject to the caprices of Major Turner, the officer in charge, and Richard Turner, inspector of the prison. It was among the rules that no one should go within three feet of the windows, a rule which seemed to be general in all Southern prisons of this character, and which their frequently-crowded state rendered peculiarly severe and difficult to serve. The manner in which the regulation was enforced was unjustifiably and wantonly cruel. Often by accident, or unconsciously, an officer would go near a window, and be instantly shot at without warning. The reports of sentries' muskets were heard almost every day, and frequently a prisoner fell, either killed or wounded."

It was to this place of torture that Lieutenant Ketcham, scarcely convalescent from his recent severe illness, was consigned by his rebel captors. Thrown into one of the crowded rooms, he contracted the fever so common and so fatal to our soldiers. Without nourishment, without medicine, and debilitated in frame, he sank, day by day, with his miserable comrades. He suffered all that could be endured with life, where life itself was suffering.

Starvation added its horrors to pain and exposure. An officer's daily ration was a small loaf of bread, about the size of a man's fist, and made of Indian meal. It weighed a little over half a pound. With it was given a piece of beef, weighing two ounces. Speaking of the allowance, its kind and quality, an officer remarked, long afterwards—"I would gladly have preferred the horse-feed in my father's stable."

But, poor and insufficient as was the general allowance, it became worse, if possible, during the time that Lieutenant Ketcham was a prisoner. About the time of his capture, the corn-bread of Libby Prison, according to testimony elicited from prisoners, "began to be of the roughest and coarsest description. Portions of the cob and husk were often found ground in with the meal. The crust was so thick and hard that the prisoners called it iron-clad To render the bread eatable, they grated it, and made mush of it, but the crust they could not grate. Now and then, after long intervals, often of many weeks, a little meat was given them, perhaps two or three mouthfuls. At a later period, they received a pint of black peas with some vinegar, every week. The peas were often full of worms, or maggots in a chysalis state, which, when they made soup, floated on the surface."

Such was the condition, such were the food and surroundings, of our officers in Libby Prison. Into the midst of the famishing multitude John Ketcham was thrust, and it was not singular that he speedily succumbed to the fever.

Three weeks, after his consignment to Libby Prison, our young lieutenant lingered amidst its horrors; three weeks of bodily prostration and mental anguish. No loving mother was there to press with her gentle hand his burning forehead, or to administer a draught to his parched lips. No voice of affection, no presence of kindred, solaced the dying youth; but his faith remained firm in the cause of his country, and he died, at last, "to make men free."

The Colonel of John's regiment was DI CES- NOLA, that gallant commander who, in the fierce fight of Aldie, received as a gift the sword of his leader, KILPATRICK, and who, charging soon after, at the head of his men, fell desperately wounded, and was captured by the enemy. In Libby Prison, this noble officer was still confined, when his young subaltern was brought in a pris- oner. He was with him to the end of his brief probation, and in a letter to the mother, after all was over, bore testimony to the merits of her departed son.

"Lieutenant Ketcham was a brave young officer, and once out of 'this,' I meant to promote him; but GOD has promoted him to a better rank!"

John was transferred, at the last hour, from "Libby" to the hospital; too late to save him, even had a rebel hospital been the place for succor. He survived his removal a day, and then followed his brother to that peace which the world knows not and can never give. Through the care of his colonel, and other friends, his body was subsequently exhumed from its temporary grave, and conveyed to his childless mother. All that is mortal of the two brothers now rests in that quiet little " God's acre"—the Friends' Burial Ground, at Milton, in Ulster County, N. Y., where two white monuments, side by side, have been raised in memory of a mother's gifts to her country.

It is the Record of these young soldiers, that they—performed their duty.

Their Fame belongs to the Republic, in whose service they died, and in whose story they will always live.

FAME, of itself, and alone, is not by any means the "be-all and the end all" of human merit or endeavor. Brave aspirations and achievements are but the index and incentive toward higher and worthier accomplishment. The Past and the Present are lessons for the Future.

Fame is nought to either of the two brothers whose story we have read. Fame is no recompense to him whose spirit has passed from the scenes of his trials and triumphs. Earthly immortality can be nought to one whose soul ascends into eternal life. It is to the future of humanity that Renown belongs, as an incentive to virtue and a stimulus to courage. David, the shepherd-lad of Israel, acting upon ages by the example of his transmitted story, has inspired, I doubt not, the striplings of numberless valleys, to dare and conquer Goliahs of oppression. Scipio and Cato and either Brutus survive, through all years, as illustrations of patriotism. For themselves their fame is as nothing; for the world and the future it may be priceless.

It is good, then, to glean in the fields of Past and Present, for all scattered ears of that golden corn which is reaped toward a mighty hereafter. While history garners its sheaves of chieftains and leaders, it lets fall, too often, the heroes of obscurity, and their brave examples perish from among us. It is good, then, to glean after History.

And here let me invoke the glorified host of nameless men, who have fallen upon the marches and battle-fields of Freedom! Here let me apostrophize the unknown armies of martyrs who have laid down their lowly lives for Liberty, in every era and upon every soil!

O! dumb and traceless shades! O! misty semblances of humanity! receding into the dimness of immemorial centuries! Ye multitudes, whose weary journeyings left no footprints, and whose fall awoke no echo! Was it your destiny to be barren of fruit for the future? to be absorbed, as clouds, into the ocean of time, leaving no reflex of your transit upon earth or in the heavens?

I think that my soul can recognize a sweet response to its invocation; a voiceless yet intelligible reply, down-flowing, as from choirs of invisible spirits, in harmonies that interpret both Past and Present. I fancy that those misty darknesses which enshroud the heroes, and patriots, and martyrs, of forgotten generations, have opened, sometimes, into vistas of immortal glory, revealing glimpses of the great White Throne; and that, out from the overpowering splendor, unsyllabled music glides into my heart, as of blessed ones chanting eternally:

" Clouds we are!" they sing—"but clouds are footstools for The Infinite. Clouds we are! but clouds of witnesses! testifying forevermore in heaven, as we testified on earth, the hope, the promise, and the assurance, of Freedom to Humanity!"

Let us leave with Our Father in Heaven the records which Earth has lost. They rest in celestial archives. Enough for us to cherish the examples that descend from our fathers, and to multiply them, by thoughts and deeds, that shall be memorials for our children hereafter.

WORDS SPOKEN AT THE BURIAL.

BY REV. O. B. FROTHINGHAM.

WORDS SPOKEN AT THE BURIAL.

BY REV. O. B. FROTHINGHAM.

FRIENDS: I have come here to-day as to a sacred place ; as a pilgrim comes to a shrine. I have come to visit the home of the noble young man whose remains are coffined here, to see the spot where he lived, the house where he was born, the mother who held him to her bosom, the neighbors and friends he loved. I have come to receive a lesson, not to give one ; to be taught, not to teach ; to be comforted, not to comfort. Better than any speech of mine is the silent thought on these relics, and on all they have passed through, since the stalwart and beautiful frame to which they belonged left your peaceful hills for the camp and the battle-field. What a strange history for such a man! Beaten up and down by all the storms of war, borne hither and thither by the changeful movement of the army, blackened by the sun and bleached by the frost, exposed to all the mutations of the weather, pinched with hunger, stiffened with cold, drenched with dew and rain, hardened by toil, wasted by fever, watching in the saddle, sleeping on the ground, begrimed by smoke and powder, a mark for sabre-cut and for rifle-ball, sick in hospital, captive in prison, dying among enemies, buried, with no shroud but his cloak, in hostile soil, lifted from the ground, coffined and brought hither at last, to repose in peace by the side of his elder brother, and in sight of the doorway through which he had so often passed; this body tells a touching and solemn story of toil, fatigue, suffering, peril, and death; but also of patience, fortitude, bravery, cheerfulness, the devotion of a generous, pure and earnest heart.

I cannot utter words of common consolation here. There are all the usual consolations, and more. There is the thought of the Infinite God, just and loving—of the kind and tender Providence, which allows nothing to be wasted, which picks up the fragments of our broken existence, ties together the loose threads of our activity, arranges our life-plan, makes good the imperfection of our labor, and perfects itself in our weakness, suffering not even the little ones to perish, and permitting no good hope to fail; there is the thought of a vast hereafter, where every life shall be made complete. These consolations are for all in ordinary times; for those whose friends are cut off by untimely accident, if we may speak of untimeliness or accident in this world of God's; for those whose dear ones die of their own ignorance, error, foolishness, and vice. For these friends of ours we have more than this; the sympathy of a great multitude, the fellowship of an immense company of noble mourners, the tender respect and love of strangers, the recognition of a country, the unspoken, perhaps unconscious, gratitude of those ready to perish. The memory of such a career, of such a character, is alone consolation sufficient for more than ordinary grief. What greater comfort could there be for a mother than to have had even one such son? To be recognized and honored as the mother of such? To live in their reflected light and glory? When I think of mothers I know, who sit mourning for boys cut off in their prime by some fate which finished their career before their career had well begun; when I think of other mothers, who sit mourning for beautiful boys who have dug their own graves by dissipation; and of other mothers yet, who are ready to pray kind death to take their boys away from temptation before they sink under it, body and soul; this widowed mother, sitting by two such graves as these, with a heart full of such memories, seems to be blessed above the rest; yes, above thousands whose sons are living at their side.

A friend, last summer, read me a letter from a young man in the army of the Potomac, written to his mother after the battle of Chancellorville. It was the elder brother of him whose remains lie here. Early in the war the hearts of both burned to take part in the conflict for what they believed to be the cause of liberty, truth, and justice among men. The elder went; the younger stayed, to support and comfort his mother. Presently came brave letters from the camp, telling of the life there, presenting the most encouraging aspects of it, for the sake of the dear ones at home, making light of the privations, hardships and perils, and showing how the pure purpose of the heart was deepening, how the manly character was ripening, under circumstances that are usually considered to be fatal to all sweetness and tenderness of nature. The soul of the younger brother was stirred by these words from the camp and the field. He felt that he must go. His mother pleads, his brother remonstrates, saying what such a man would say about duty at home, the mother's loneliness, the chances of battle, and the fearful thing it would be were both to die—but saying too, in an undertone which was felt, not seen in the writing—"Well, it is a great cause, and good men are needed in it, and it is no wonder that every high-minded man is eager to do his part." And John followed Edward; left the hills, the homestead, the farm, the sorrowing mother, the delights of his quiet, tranquil life.

Letters came now from both boys; letters that suggested—though their writers knew nothing of it and did not suspect it—the good they must be doing in the camp by their courage, their obedience, their high tone of loyalty, not less by the purity and temperance and manly simplicity of their example. Brave we knew they were; ready, faithful, unflinching, unmurmuring. At Gettysburg the elder brother falls. The younger searches the bloody miles of battle-ground for the body, finds it after many hours among the slain, bears it in his arms a mile to a quiet resting-place, whence it is removed to be borne northward by tender hands, and laid, in the gorgeous mid-summer, beneath the trees he loved so well.

Letters now from one brother again, telling the bereaved mother that he was unhurt and well; that he should come back to her soon ; that Edward's spirit was about him and would ward off the balls; and in the future would be about them both, and help them along the rest of their way.

But exposure, work, sorrow, brought sickness ; weeks of miserable sickness in the hospital, a sigh for the invigorating breath of these hills, and for a cheering sight of his old friends. But the bugle was ringing outside; his brave fellows were making ready for the charge ; he leaves the hospital, full of courage as ever, but too feeble in body to take the field ; for a fortnight, daily, he is out, wrapped in smoke and dust; narrowly escaping from death, as he rallies his men, he is taken prisoner. Still, from the horrible Richmond prison, come the letters, brave and uncomplaining ; he is unwounded, he is safe now from danger in battle ; he has strength to bear him through ; he needs but a few comforts, blankets, clothing ; he is not treated harshly. Poor fellow! he is dying from exhaustion. He goes to the hospital for a few days ; he goes in the afternoon; the next morning he is dead in his bed.

It was long before this brother found his way homeward; the mother's heart was getting tired with waiting; but he is here at last; and we are here, to be honored by the presence of his remains.

For what was this young life given away? For what were this sweet home, this pleasant existence, these tranquil pursuits, this dear mother resigned? For what were all these cares and toils and sorrows borne? Not for himself; not that he might be richer, greater, more famous; not in pride or vindictiveness, or young love of adventure; but that the poor blacks of the South, whom he knew not, and who knew not him—the poor blacks, to whom the very name of man had been denied—the beaten, treated as the offscouring of the earth, might have their human rights; for these, whom he never saw, he died, with a faith as simple and a devotion as pure as ever man had, counting what he did as little, remembering only what he ought to do. Unpretending, unambitious, with the heart of a little child and the conscience of a Christian man, he lived and died for a principle.

It is a strange sight, the coffin of a soldier, wrapped in a battle-flag, lying in a Friends' meeting-house. He was educated a Friend, and was in spirit, to the end, one of that peaceful brotherhood, who abhor violence, and blood-shedding, and war. Comfort yourselves, oh, Friends! with the thought that he preserved that pious abhorrence as sacredly as you do. He was a lover of peace; he went out in the holy cause of peace, as a peacemaker. Not to make war or to continue war, but to put an end to war; to die himself, if need were, by the hand of war, that war might cease. To make war in his country forever impossible, by eradicating human slavery, its permanent cause, he took up arms. There seemed no other way of doing it. He would thankfully have used other means, had other means been permitted. Accepting these, he prayed always for the quiet rest he hoped these would bring. You need not be afraid of shocking your principles by receiving him here from battle. His spirit would do no violence to the saintliest communion. Do we hate war less in these days than formerly? Nay, friends, we hate it, if possible, a thousand times more, and we hate slavery ten thousand times more, when we see them, father and son, doing such deeds as this.

O, my friends, the time is coming, the time is surely coming, when all they who went down into this great struggle will be held in honor by all lovers of order and peace; when they who have lost arm or leg in it will be looked at with profound respect; when they who have come out of it riven or scarred will be counted among the beautiful; when they who, like this young man, have died in it, with a noble sense of its significance, will be reckoned among the martyrs of God's truth. The time will come, when they who have sent husband, son, brother, lover, into this struggle, will be cherished in grateful remembrance. Yes, when they who have suffered in it, in any wise, even with no high sentiment of its grandeur, and no high purpose in their death, will yet be wrapped about with its sanctifying glory. Then we, who have done nothing, who have but given a few of our superfluous dollars, who have but preached what others ought to do, will apologize for our well-preserved health and beauty, and will be glad to hide our shame behind the form of some hero of our blood.

It is sad to see so much young manhood laid low in its bloom, and laid low by that barbarian, War, pushed on by his more loathsome brother— Slavery. But we must not be narrow in judging the issues of a human life. Who can tell how existence may be most profitably spent? Who can decide what is the most effectual doing? Providence decides all that for us, and makes every earnest man do his work, wherever he is, and whether he live longer or shorter. Had our young friend lived, he would have been known and beloved among these hills, and, doubtless, would have made the force of his character felt by his neighbors. A good son, a faithful friend, a useful townsman, a sincere, honest, humane man, he would have lived and died here, in the quiet, and the little stream of his existence would have fed the moral life of his generation, only as one of your mountain rivulets feeds the Atlantic Ocean. The heroic quality in him would have slumbered ; his power of sacrifice would have been uncalled for, his example of pure patriotism would have been lost. Now he is known by many, to whom personally he was a stranger. He is respected and loved by some who never would have heard of him. He has exhibited manly qualities of the highest order, where men could see them. He has shed a virtue abroad in the camp. He has read lessons of duty to some whom he would hardly have thought of instructing. For my own part, though I never saw him, I gratefully confess my debt to him for a fresh belief in the nobleness of nature, for a more living faith in man, for a fresh conviction of the worth of a simple fidelity to principle, for a new sense of the sublimity of sacrifice. For me he has done much by his living, and by his dying. Yes, O my brother! they tell me that words of mine helped to show you the significance of this struggle, and did something to deepen in your heart the purpose that has brought you thus early to the grave. You have richly repaid the debt. You have shown me the significance of a good man's deed, and, I hope, have deepened in my heart a purpose that will help me to nobler life.

But we have said too much, we have broken too long and too impertinently the sacred silence. We should have allowed him to speak more. Had he been able to speak, he would have rebuked us for praising what he did in the sincerity of his heart, because he could not help it, and under pain of self-condemnation had he left it undone. Let us lay what is left of his poor body in the ground, and think of him as living and working on ; for in the future time, when sweet peace shall come back to us, he will live and work in the pure sentiments he has aided in strengthening, and in the noble institutions he has died to establish.

THE END.

www.ingramcontent.com/pod-product-compliance
Lightning Source LLC
Chambersburg PA
CBHW032145010726
47493CB00008BA/2584